KITCHENER PUBLIC LIBRARY

3 9098 02061750 1

D1441127

DATING THE UNDEAD
loving the immortal man

Laura Ross Managing Editor
Chris Lorette David Designer
Eric Harvey Brown Photo Editor
Katherine Furman Copy Chief

Produced by **The Stonesong Press, LLC**
Judy Linden Vice President, Executive Editor
Ellen Scordato Partner, Production Manager

ACKNOWLEDGMENTS

To **Kristen Painter,** the amazing author of *Blood Rights* and
an invaluable resource to all things paranormal!

To **Judy Linden, Ellen Scordato, Laura Ross,
Deb Brody,** and **Margo Lipschultz,** for the reads,
the insight, and the suggestions!

To **Deidre Knight** for always being in our corner!

To **the husbands who shall remain nameless,** for sliding the food under
the door after we locked ourselves in the cave to meet our deadlines!

Jill: I'd like to thank Gena Showalter.

Gena: I was going to thank you. Now I look like I'm copying you.

Jill: Well, I can't help it that I'm more considerate and thought of it first.

Gena: You just said it first. Anyway. I'd like to thank Jill Monroe.

Jill: You always have to have the last word.

Gena: Word.

ISBN-13: 978-0-373-89252-5

© 2012 by Gena Showalter and Jill Monroe

G'ORÉAL

HE MAY BE UNDEAD— BUT YOU'RE NOT!

When you're dating an immortal, the fun begins when the sun goes down— and your skin tone may be paying the price. Get rid of that ghostly pallor and regain the LG glow he loves, with SKIN-COLORING PRODUCTS from G'Oréal.

Featuring shades designed to attract your *special* kind of guy, G'Oréal's unique line of SKIN-COLORING PRODUCTS is sure to turn up the heat at any hour. Just apply evenly in the morning, then nap the day away. By the time the sun goes down, you'll be toned to tasty perfection.

Our model is wearing Angelic Ivory

G'ORÉAL

SKIN-COLORING PRODUCT

ANGELIC IVORY

G'ORÉAL
SKIN-COLORING PRODUCT
DEMONIC BRONZE

G'ORÉAL
SKIN-COLORING PRODUCT
ZOMBIE BABY-BLUE

G'ORÉAL
SKIN-COLORING PRODUCT
VAM-PALE

IN THIS ISSUE

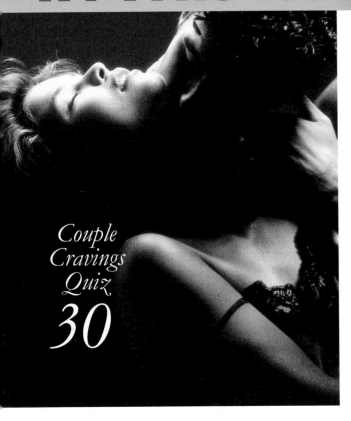

Couple Cravings Quiz
30

Killer Cocktails
132

Strangers in the Night **10**

HIS & HERS (& ITS)

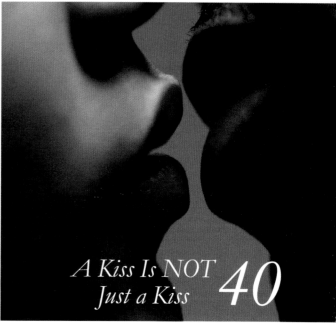

A Kiss Is NOT Just a Kiss 40

Is It Hot in This Dungeon— or Is It YOU? 62

Howlin' Hot Fashion Makeovers
67

Unique Gifts
72

Real-Life Lords of the Underworld Bare All!
104

Angel in the Kitchen
126

Money, Honey!
138

Immorstrology
156

So . . . you're dating the undead, and you have lots of questions, opinions, and very special dilemmas. Good thing there's a magazine *just for you,* right? *Dating the Undead* is dedicated to those who dream of a fling, a close encounter, a long-term relationship, or a . . . whatever with a hot man of the otherworld. We've gathered experts (including a few of those immortals) in all areas to offer tips, guidance, inspiration, inside information—and fun—from the other side. In short, we try to answer all of the questions you Living Girls (LGs for short) have been (metaphorically) dying to ask!

Will a Vampire burst into flames in the sunlight, or will he glitter?
(Neither!)

How many dateless nights are ahead of me since my Werewolf boyfriend is part of a pack—and I'm not?
(Not many, if he's a keeper!)

Are all Dragon-Shifters ticklish under their scales, or just mine?
(Depends. Is your Dragon a land- or water-dweller?)

How do I break my Zombie out of his shy shell so I can introduce him to my friends?
(Two words: *time* and *patience.*)

Just how naughty can I be before I shock my Angel?
(Not very, unfortunately. But the good news is, a shock might be just what he needs!)

Does horn size indicate the size of anything else on my Demon?
(Hell to the yes!)

Some of these creatures don't breathe, but they certainly take *our* breath away.

The movies may have brought these legendary supermen to life, but we promise you there's more to your fabulous immortal than hypnotic eyes, washboard abs, eternal stamina, and a willingness to take a bullet for you (and recover in time to take you out on the town). *Dating the Undead* exists to put the myths about him to bed (and *him* to bed with *you,* if that's where you want him to be), as well as providing the real deal about his habits, desires, weaknesses, turn-ons, and soft spots.

So, if you fear looking at 27 coffins instead of 27 dresses, check out "Angelic Etiquette for Modern Gals and Ghouls," where you'll learn critical dos and don'ts.

Maybe you loved your Demon's partying ways—at first— but now you're just in hell and ready for a change. How do you lose an immortal in ten days when he's going to live forever? Check out "Undead—and Gone!"

On the flip side, how do you lure that luscious immortal when he refuses to date outside his species? Our quick tips for attracting his attention will help you bring home the Victory (or whatever his name happens to be).

Even if you've only flirted with the idea of dating an immortal, every article in this month's issue has something to offer you. Because, really, speaking LG to LG, we've all occasionally wished our mortal guy had a Vampire's ability to stay up all night (wink, wink) or a Dragon's knack for setting our blood on fire. And while it's true that—just like their flesh-and-blood counterparts—immortals can be brooding, ruthless, and inflexible, they're also oh, so sexy . . . and each one of them is looking for his soul mate.

Are you the right woman to answer his call? We think so. Enjoy this journey into the thrilling world of true paranormal romance. Along the way, you might just discover a love to last the ages. Oh, you lucky LGs!

Yours forever,

Dena Showalter

and

Jill Monroe

LGs Speak!

Dear DTU,

Here's our pick of this month's letters from readers. Got a question, a comment, or a thorny pet peeve about your immortal? We're all ears!

I'm an LG who's never liked the idea of dating a Shifter, but last month's article, "Pick of the Litter," really helped me see the Werewolves in a different light. They might be hairy, and their bite might be far worse than their bark, but in the end, they're only looking for love—just like me.
Tonya
New York, NY

I'm a little . . . overweight. Okay, a lot overweight. And I never thought a sexy immortal could be into me. But your summer issue helped me find the perfect swimsuit for my curves and the best beach to showcase them. Two days into my vacation, I'd bagged and tagged my new Dragon boyfriend—and he thinks I'm smoking hot just the way I am!
Cara
Seattle, WA

While I appreciate your willingness to explore all avenues of life (and death), referring to Werewolves as "moondoggies" and Vampires as "hemogoblins" was crossing a line. Do you like it when other species refer to us humans as "meat bags?" I don't think so!
Anonymous

You guys clearly know nothing about Zombies, otherwise you never would have encouraged your readers to take them home to meet Mom and Dad. My ultra-shy Zom was miserable the entire night and barely spoke to anyone. He didn't even eat the mac-and-headcheese my mother made especially for him! To get him back to his sweet, old self, I had to take him to a video arcade and run through half a paycheck's worth of quarters, which was fun, I'll admit . . . but still.

Please advise caution when LGs attempt to crack a Zom-boy out of his shell.
Rita
Amarillo, TX

Thank you for being unafraid to say it's okay to date a Demon. I've always been the good girl, and let's face it, he's actually from hell, but I've crushed on him *forever*. After reading "Seductive Sins He Wants You to Commit" I finally had the courage to approach him and ask him out. He said no (I guess he didn't read the article) but I don't regret asking. Nothing ventured, nothing gained. Here's hoping there's a more willing creature in my future!
Jessica
Madison, WI

Strangers in the Night

Who are they—and what do they really want?

Immortals. They are the bad boys we hope to tame, the good boys we can bring home to Mom, and the adventure we've been craving, all wrapped up in one delicious package. We simply can't get enough of them. But good looks, money, and power aside, what do we really know about them (besides the fact that they aren't the only ones interested in a little nibbling)?

We at *DTU* did our homework, and we consider it our duty (and pleasure) to share what we learned with our readers. So listen up as we break down their strengths and weaknesses and help you understand those sexy men of the otherworld you're lusting after—and what you'll have to deal with if you want to win one's undying love.

What's up with **VAMPIRES**?

Vampires have slightly chilled skin, mesmerizing eyes, and fangs that release a pleasurable chemical while biting. The only thing they "eat" is human blood. Unlike the mythic creatures portrayed in books and movies, they will not burst into flames or glitter if they step into the sunlight. However, they *are* sensitive to bright lights and do burn easily. On the plus side, sensitive skin has hundreds of erogenous zones, the most notable being the ropes of muscle on his stomach, the sexy curve of his lower back (often overlooked), and the tempting trail up his inner thigh.

As for creation, Vampires are made, not born. A mortal's blood is drained by fang to the point of death, and then he or she is fed from the maker's own vein. This is not necessarily a consensual act (though always a sensual one, at least for the maker). Survival mostly arises from the Vampire's deep-seated instinct to defeat the grave, and the process is not without traumatic circumstances. Sometimes, a newly minted Vampire will go into a killing rage aimed at his or her maker or suffer death-long guilt that they must prey upon human blood for their continued existence. (That's where Vamp therapists come in.)

Vampires often feel a sense of superiority toward mortals for their frailty, but more often than not, this is to disguise a deep-rooted yearning to enjoy the pleasures of being human, such as feeling the warmth of the sun without pain or the tastes of sweet and tart.

Something to note: Until a Vampire reaches the age of 300, he is considered a Vampling and is required to clear all major life choices with the American Vampire Council (AVC). These include marriage, adopting a child, and moving to another country.

What's up with **WEREWOLVES?**

Many myths surround the creation of the Werewolf. Some legends suggest that a seventh son is destined to become Were. Other stories say they were created by God to battle Demons. While no one knows their original source, Werewolves have lived among humans for hundreds of years and can be created in two ways: by birth to werewolf parents or by bite.

While in human form, Were-Shifters are notable for their extraordinary height and muscle mass. While in wolf form, they are still tall, still muscled, and the color of their fur will perfectly match that of their human hair. In both forms, they have claws, a fierce temper, and love to growl, all of which can be frightening. And don't say we didn't warn you about keeping Demons and Werewolves separate. (Maybe there is something to that Werewolf battling Demon legend.)

On the plus side, they are almost always up for a cuddle. Be careful, though, as they are extremely territorial and have been known to "mark" their girlfriends with their teeth or claws.

Werewolves by birth enjoy the benefit of living in a pack and are guided by many Shifters as they approach their first change. However, wolves created by bite often suffer immense pain and confusion . . . if they live. These dark loners are often prickly, but once they determine that you accept and love them for who they are, you're mated for life.

Something to note: A Were can be a perfect choice for girls who embrace the "natural" look. These furry hunks won't mind if you ditch your razor.

What's up with **DRAGONS?**

Dragon-Shifters: Most of these muscle men are brunettes—blonds and red-heads are a rarity—and they are even taller and more broad-shouldered than Werewolves. When they shift, they acquire a snout, jowls, scales, wings as fierce as a Demon's, and tails. With their saliva, they can create and spew fire. Maybe that's why they are best known for their hot tempers! Yet, despite those passionate outbursts, their instincts to protect those they love prevent them from becoming (too) destructive.

If you really want to irritate a Dragon, suggest that he popped out of an egg! (Perhaps that hurts because it hits so close to home!) As the story goes, humans and Dragons battled so fiercely that the fiery creatures neared extinction. But then two families, one Dragon and one human, got together and

decided that their only means of mutual survival was to pair off their children. Some legends have it that the woman was human and the man a Dragon, while others state the reverse. Whichever it was, the two beings fell in love. The human admired the Dragon for its strength and honor and the Dragon grew fond of the human for its compassion and intelligence. And very soon, Dragon-Shifters were born.

Something to note: Pure Dragons no longer live (that we know of). New Shifters are created only the old-fashioned (and really fun) way. Believe us when we say these winged warriors feel a sense of urgency to propagate the species. Dragons prefer to live either in caves or surrounded by water. For some reason, the cave-dwellers are always ticklish.

What's up with **ZOMBIES?**

Younger Zombies have a lovely blue-tinged skin, while older ones tend to have a smooth pearl-gray hue. Their eyes are black and their bodies vary in size and shape. They will eat anything, but particularly enjoy all of those calorie-filled delicious goodies that the killjoys of the world say are not good for us. They love to watch TV and play video games, and if you aren't careful, they will do so ad nauseam. The good news is that they are great listeners, rarely argue, and make the perfect mate for the homebody LG who likes the strong, silent type.

If you're an LG reading this and definitely not a Zombie, then you have nothing to fear from this particular immortal (yes, we know what your mother has told you—but she's wrong). If you're up to date on your immunizations, you're officially immune to the virus that caused so many humans to change in centuries past. So go ahead, nibble on your Zombie boyfriend (or him on you)!

Something to note: Zombies like nothing better than a practical joke. Where do you think the whole Zombies-hunting-humans legend came from? Somewhere, some Zombie is laughing his head off . . . literally. (See? Another joke!) What is not a laughing matter is their fear of oceans. Perhaps the salt burns their skin, or perhaps they're afraid of sharks. Whatever the reason, this means absolutely no skinny-dipping—except in hotel pools, that is.

What's up with **ANGELS?**

Angels are oh-so-delectable good boys with skin touched by the sun and faces so lovely you will literally tear up just from looking at them. The color of their eyes and wings ranges from the palest gold to the darkest black, and if they have a flaw, it is that they are sometimes, well, too perfect. In every way. As you can imagine, this can be annoying—but you might find it worth dealing with. What they lack in a sense of humor and playfulness, they make up for with their honesty and willingness to forgive and forget. And be ready to gently coax your Angel into bed. They don't have a lot of experience and can be a little inhibited at first, but if you channel their need to please in the right direction, you'll find them worth the effort.

Some of the Angels walking among us are considered "fallen," but even they are not one hundred percent bad boy (and never really will be—unless they choose to go Demon). They have been stripped of their heavenly duties and tend to be confused about their role among us. We know you can help your fallen one find purpose, and we hope you do—because the world probably doesn't need another Demon.

Something to note: When an Angel falls in love, it's forever. You will become the reason he exists. There is no such thing as divorce to an Angel. So, if wingers are your thing, choose wisely! Also, many Angels are able to read human minds. Others can compel humans to speak the truth or even to admit to every wrong they've ever committed. To them, this can sometimes pass as foreplay. To you? Maybe not so much.

Finally, let's turn our attention to Demons. History is pretty clear on how Demons were made: by their own choice. These naughty boys are fallen Angels who, having been stripped of their heavenly duties, have completely disavowed all things "good" and signed up for the dark side. There are over a dozen different types of Demons, but we'll stick to the two most prevalent.

What's up with FIRE DEMONS?

Fire Demons are drop-dead handsome bad boys who look human until they experience strong emotion. With arousal, anger, sadness, and even joy, glittering scales cover their skin, their eyes glow a bright, mesmerizing red, and bull-like horns sprout from their heads. Be careful, because those horns often drip with poison. Not all Fire Demons possess wings, but those who do have one thing in common—razor-sharp edges. These wild guys like to party like rock stars and are always up for an adventure. While they can't be counted on for the long term (until the mating craze overtakes them), they can guarantee a lack of inhibition in bed and real staying power every time.

What's up with ICE DEMONS?

Like their fiery brothers, Ice Demons are gorgeous, bad to the nth degree, and affected by their emotions, but they do not produce scales or poisoned horns. What you will find is skin that morphs into the color and temperature of a frozen lake. Cerulean, pure, and did we mention gorgeous? Their eyes become electric blue, though you might find shimmers of green and silver. They are, by far, the most beautiful of all the races (at least to these LGs), and their attraction factor surpasses even that of the Angels. These icy Romeos are taller and more muscular than any other Demonic sub-species. There are times they cannot even touch human skin without leaving ice burns—or freezing the body altogether—but really, this won't cool a determined woman down.

Something to note: The "mating craze" is something both the Fire and Ice Demons experience, but only once in their lives and only for one specific woman. This drive bonds them to the female, effectively wedding the pair for eternity. ❖

Everything you need to turn that lair, dungeon, or den into a comfortable and chic home for two—and our prices are out of this world!

Cave&Coffin

PARTY ANIMALS

As always, we're hitting the hot spots with Nancy O'Hell— our favorite LG Queen of the Night.

What with two full moons, it's been *quite* a month for parties—and ladies, I am proud to say I managed to make it to every one of them without losing my day job at the blood bank.

First stop was the annual Vampire Ball, and yes, I agreed to be one of the hors d'oeuvres. My instructions were simple: wear a bikini, remain on top of the buffet table, and offer a nice juicy vein to anyone with fangs. Well, I was nervous, and the Angeltini I hoped would calm me down went straight to my head. It also went to the head of the first Vampire who bit me. He spent the rest of the night swinging from the chandeliers! I don't want to be indiscreet, so I won't mention any names . . . but which suspiciously pale Australian movie star married to a country singer do you suppose ended up waltzing out of there with a Vamp on each arm? Hmm . . . that might explain why she never ages. (And you thought it was Botox!)

Moving on . . . the following week I hit the opening of a brand-new dance club frequented by the hottest Demons on the planet. (You can spot a few of them in the ads on these pages.) It's called Hellfyre and let me tell you, it is ultra-exclusive. Even if you can find it (good luck getting a cab to take you to the corner of Gore and Mayhem), it's pretty tough to get past the Dragons at the door—unless you're a luscious LG ready to party, that is. Once inside, I danced the night away—Demons really know how to show a girl a good time. The music was provided by DJ

Bloodsquirt, and the special cocktail was the Howler, made of Absolut Cranberry with a splash of Wolfbane. After a few of those, and hours of dancing under a neon flame-show that totally replicated hell (but without the torment and damnation)—phew!— I was ready to crawl home and sleep through a few lunar cycles. Oh, wait— I know you are dying to hear about the celebrities I spotted there. My faithful readers know how much I love to speculate about who might be undead but still in the closet about it. Well . . . how's this for a scoop? Corner booth in the VIP section, nibbling on a pretty young neck like there was no tomorrow—none other than James Franco! Makes perfect sense when you think about it, right?

There's one other smashing event I can't resist sharing with you, and that is last week's Killer Fiends concert. I wasn't dying (as it were) to go, but my bestie insisted on dragging me. At first it was all noise to me, and getting knocked around by the crowd sucked. I hated it—until my eyes locked onto the lead singer. Ladies, he was the dreamiest Zombie I'd ever seen. Our instant connection was so intense, the rest of the world faded away and I actually found myself dancing, screaming, and cheering for encores. After the show, I used my charm (and thigh-high black leather stiletto boots) to get backstage, where the band was relaxing after the show. I shoved a few lame little Angel groupies out of the way and headed straight for Jonas Jones, the afore-

mentioned Fiends front man. "Hey, gorgeous!" he said to me. "Thanks for giving me somebody really special to sing to tonight. Why don't you join us for some beers, Doritos, and video games?" Readers, what can I say? It was a magical night—and I am now a fan of Zombie Rock. Next time you run into me on the street, ask me to show you my new tattoo—it bears a striking resemblance to a certain lead singer with a killer smile (and a bit of nacho cheese in his front teeth)!

Until next month, girls, party like you might die tomorrow! (Hey, you never know. You could get lucky.)

Eternal Kisses,

Are They Undead?

We've snapped your favorite celebrities and we have to wonder, are they living or . . . UN?

Who doesn't love Captain Jack Sparrow, aka Johnny Depp? No matter the part he plays, his pale sensuality always manages to enrapture us—and he certainly brought a blood-mongering relish to the role of Sweeney Todd, didn't he? The ladies love him for his burning intensity and his (superhuman?) energy both on and off the screen. The word is, this seductive night owl takes his naps in a bed with a lid. Now, the only question in our minds is whether or not that bed sleeps two. . . .

Others with Vamp Potential: Angelina Jolie, James Franco, Tom Cruise, Iman, Al Pacino, Olivia Wilde

Okay, it doesn't take a genius to figure out that Gerard Butler has a bit of the teasing Werewolf in him. With his I-want-to-play-with-you grin, that mischievous twinkle in his eyes, and his—we're just gonna say it—roguish love of the ladies, we think this acclaimed actor is howling every chance he gets. The last time he walked the red carpet, we're pretty sure there was a full moon . . . 'nuff said?

Others with Werewolf Potential: Christopher Walken, Mickey Rourke, Zach Galifanakis, Penn Badgley, Tom Brady, Will Smith, Helena Bonham Carter, Juliette Lewis, Brad Pitt

Hey, Vince Vaughn: undead much? If it's true that we are what we eat, then this beautiful, affable actor has been dining on brains and funny bones. He definitely knows how to reel us in without having to chase! Even when he's couch potatoing (yes, we just made that a verb) his sharp wit is always on display. His goofy smile, his shambling gait, his crumb-covered jeans . . . we can't help loving this easygoing charmer. And we can't help thinking there's something a little bit Zombie about this picture.

Others with Zombie Potential: Ben Stiller, Anna Faris, Kristen Wiig, Michael Clarke Duncan, Seth Rogen, Will Farrell, Adam Sandler, John Heder, Horatio Sanz, John Cho

You follow their careers and their love lives. You see their movies, buy their music, and stay up late to watch them on *Conan*. You even know the names of their adopted children and the number of times they've been in rehab. But here's something you don't know for sure. Are they . . . human?

You're an LG with a taste for out-of-this-world guys—so it makes sense that the celebrities who fascinate you the most might just have a little something special. We've been studying the situation, and we've come up with some prime suspects. Are these stars on the down-low about their immortality? You decide.

Hello, Angel face! Blair Underwood might just be one of the most enduringly yummy stars in the Hollywood firmament—let's face it, he's downright heavenly. Whether he's flashing his pearly whites on TV or proving he has a heart of gold with his charity work, there's a radiance emanating from Blair that makes us feel all warm inside. Angelic? Definitely. Bona fide Angel? Could be.

Others with Angel Potential: Ryan Reynolds, Jude Law, Jennifer Lopez, Jason Momoa, Drew Barrymore, Queen Latifah, Sandra Bullock, Robert Pattinson, Justin Timberlake, Naveen Andrew

Those sexy, smoldering eyes, that insane sex appeal . . . yeah, we've suspected it for a while. This wild man has Demon written all over him (perhaps in the handwriting of his conquests)! Our first clue about his fiery status was his ability to party all night—and our second was all of those gorgeous ladies flocking to his side! We understand: no one girl can handle him, and no mere human can keep up. That won't stop us from trying!

Others with Demon Potential: Nicolas Cage, Mark Wahlberg, Jack Nicholson, Alex Pettyfer, Mila Kunis

Paging Indiana Jones! Harrison Ford has been setting our hearts on fire for decades—could it be that he's got a real flame-thrower in there? As our favorite action hero, Harrison always outraces the bad guys and saves the planet from annihilation. You can call it acting if you want to—we call it classic Dragon behavior. As he gets older he only gets sexier, and we have a feeling we will continue to burn for him throughout eternity.

Others with Dragon Potential: Leonardo DiCaprio, Naomi Campbell, Tina Fey, Steven Tyler, Lady Gaga, Michael Spears, Daniel Dae Kim ❖

STAY NIBBLING SWEET!

Dirty talk can be fun—but no immortal, no matter how long he's been undead, wants to taste a dirty mouth! Getbit Gum keeps you kissing, nibbling, gnawing, clawing sweet, whether you are petting with your Angel or doing the nasty with your Demon.

PERPETUAL CALENDAR

A Month of Immortal Events from Around the Block and Around the Globe

It's a great month for all things immortal! On the 1st, you can get some real insight into **1** → Vampire politics with the annual **American Vampire Council conference.** This year it's in Miami, so pack your sunscreen and your club-wear, because South Beach is going to get a big bite taken out of it. If you're more into Robert's Rules of Order than testing out a stripper pole, be sure to sit in on the AVC's general meeting, which is open to all, although only members are permitted to speak. Vampire politics can be very complex, but get two sexy Elders into a debate and you won't care what they're saying!

9 → The 9th brings us the **Anniversary of the Zombie Uprising.** Most major cities will host (slow-moving) parades to commemorate the event, but those in the know will be hitting the dive bars after dark for the real party.

A really entertaining event this month is the annual **Werewolf Motorcycle Rally** to raise money for the ASPCA. The rally kicks off on the 16th in Jacksonville, Florida, and ends in

New Orleans. Pit stops along the way are set up to raise additional funds while giving the participants a break to refuel and comb the bugs out of their fur. Throw on your best leather halter and swing by with checkbook in hand—you may find a stray in need of some attention.

17
18
19
20 →
21

Check your paper for dates and locations of the granddaddy of all bridal shows, **Undead & About To Be Wed,** as it tours nationwide through local convention centers. Even if you're not getting married, you won't want to miss the his-and-hers wedding night coffins, blood fountains, Vampire bat releases, and spectacular lingerie/fetish attire fashion shows. Grab a ghoul-crazy girlfriend and go. Trust us.

TGIF! Hot weather means **Fright-day Nights at the Beach** on both the Pacific and Atlantic seaboards. Every Friday brings another immortal

beachside party, and each one has its own theme—from "Gypsies, Vamps, and Thieves" (a tribute to Cher that brings out her many undead admirers) to "Earth Angel" (where mortals in heavenly garb get to mingle with the haloed ones). Vampires are especially fond of these bashes since summer nights are shorter and they have to maximize their fun hours. And of course, the Werewolves will be there to howl at even the smallest sliver of moon. Getting there early means you might catch a Dragon-Shifter or Fire Demon lighting the evening's bonfire. Hot! Literally! Be prepared for over-indulging, skinny-dipping from everyone but the Zombies, and all kinds of devastatingly handsome men. Best part? No worries about getting sunburned!

If heat's not your thing, **Frost Bite Fest** runs all month in Svalbard, Norway, made even more fun by the fact that the nearby Troll and Jotun hot springs are open all night! Check out some Night-Demon skiing, then swing by one of the many tents selling handmade arts and crafts by the local Vampire and Werewolf communities. My personal recommendation is the Divine Wine booth, selling the wares of a local Angel-owned and operated vineyard that produces some of the most heavenly vintages anywhere.

23
24
25
26
27
28
29

The end of the month brings the **Immortal Home Tour** in San Francisco. Want to see how the other half lives (and has lived for centuries)? Buy a ticket and check out some of the most amazing Victorian mansions, underground caves, and secret castles in the world, many with the original owners still in residence.

And, as always, wherever you happen to be, check the local underground papers for unusual festivals, monsters' balls, blood rituals, and undead celebrations of every kind. Have a blast! ❖

Gabrielle Gabs
Angelic Etiquette for Modern Gals and Ghouls

Gabrielle Saint Seer is best known as the founder of a nationwide network of schools for immortals in need of a little taming, known as EFF (Etiquette for Freaks). Her bestselling book, EFF You, *was a finalist for the National Book Award in the Immortal Nonfiction category, and her weekly daytime TV show,* What the Eff?, *can be seen on the AfterLifetime Network.*

Hello, my LG lovelies—may I start by saying you all look heavenly? And I should know! It has been quite a month, and I have been inundated with fascinating letters from you, asking about everything from Zombie table manners to whether it is okay to serve him red blood while you eat fish or chicken. As always, I'm here to offer support, guidance, and just a little bit of humor to take the stress out of dating an immortal. I may look like an Angel, but (like many of you on a Saturday night), I've got a little Demon in me!

●●●

Dear Gabrielle,
I am dating a super-fabulous Vampire, but I'm a modern girl, and I like to pay my own way, at least sometimes. Every time I try to reach for a check (or even order for myself), he gets offended and sulky, his fangs come out, and the romantic mood of the evening is broken. I don't want to offend him— should I just sit back and enjoy his old (OLD)-school behavior?
Signed,
Treated and Tired of It

Dear Treated,
I think there are some girls dating Zombies out there who are probably a little bit jealous of you right now, but I hear you loud and clear. Sometimes the courtly routine can be a bit overwhelming and we start to feel like our Vampire's property rather than his significant human. Just remember, he's been around so long, his first girlfriend may have been Marie Antoinette, and throughout most of history, men were expected to treat ladies like fragile Angels, not Amazons. You've come a long way, baby, but he hasn't— at least not yet. Break him in slowly by buying him small gifts, running his bath, picking out his cape. When his birthday comes (especially if it is a big one, like 500 or 1,000), suggest that you would like to treat him to a night on the town. And never reach for the check suddenly—always ask first. You wouldn't want to end up in the emergency room with a gushing wrist puncture, now would you? And if none of this works for you, here's a radical suggestion: try dating a Demon for a while. He is sure to let you pick up the check whenever you want (after he's ordered a few more drinks, that is). After a few weeks, you may come running back to your courtly Vamp.

●●●

Dear Gabrielle,
I'm going to get right to the point, because there's no delicate way to ask this. Is it okay to sleep with an immortal on the first date? I don't want to seem too . . . easy, but hoooboy, some of the Dragons I meet at parties are panty-melting hot—literally! And one kiss on the hand from a gothy Vampire makes my blood race to my most delicious parts. Let's not even talk about Werewolves, except to say that they give new meaning to the term "heavy petting."

To submit or not to submit? Help!
Signed,
Hot and Bothered

Dear Hot,
Well, you really do have your knickers in a knot, don't you? I think your imagination is racing faster than your pulse! Time to take a few deep breaths, a cold shower, and a long, hard look at your life goals. You are here because you like walking on the wild side—but I'm afraid this is one of the ways that immortals are a lot like human guys . . . they act like Mr. Right Now—but they'd rather feel like Mr. Right. If you really have long-term monster love on your mind, it's up to you to control your libido and save something for next time. Trust me, that's the best way to maintain his interest. What's your hurry? Play your cards right and you'll have all eternity to explore each other's gross anatomies!

And now, with sex on all our minds, it's time for Miss Gabrielle to offer some good old-fashioned advice about how an LG enamored of an immortal can always be on her best behavior. We love them because they're different, right? The trick is to understand those differences and rise to every occasion. Here are a few tips:

1 **Stay away from public displays of affection.** With a human, sure, go for it. But when you're dealing with an immortal, public pleasuring means more than just scratching an itch. For Vamps, a kiss in front of a crowd can be the same as uttering marriage vows. And Werewolves, well, as Mick Jagger would say, when you start them up, they never stop! (Speaking of whom . . . I think Mick has a little wolf in him, don't you? It's just a theory, but I mean—how old is that guy?) A Dragon might just turn around and singe anyone who interrupts your affectionate gesture—and that includes the waiter . . . a salesperson . . . your mom! Angels embarrass easily, so they might go into a shame spiral, and that will not lead to another date. And Demons are just too hot to handle without oven mitts. They might not stop until the very end. You get the picture: immortals like to keep things private—but behind closed doors, watch out!

2 **Find out if your immortal prefers to be the pursuer—or the pursued.** Most immortals are alphas, and as you probably know, alphas love the thrill of the hunt. And really, don't you love the thrill of being caught? Running after you, literally or figuratively, will get his heart racing and his blood flowing. However, some immortals have been chasing tail for so long they crave a change and want you to sprint after *them*. How can you tell which category your guy falls into? Well, if he's broody, moody or just plain snooty, tug on your racing shoes. You'll need to push him to the finish line.

3 **Never diss your last date to your current date—unless, of course, your ex was a mere mortal.**

When it comes to human "competition," there's nothing an undead male likes more than a good laugh. (Well, except for actually killing the competition.) But seriously, a good girl never kisses and disses.

On that note, never, ever make bedroom eyes at another man—no matter his species—while on a date with an immortal. You read the part above about killing the competition, right? If you flirt with someone else, that someone else is gonna get hurt. Fangs, claws, and fire aren't just fashion accessories, you know. And it's not like Zombies really need an excuse to dig into fresh meat. If you're thinking your Angel will forgive you anything, think again. (Speaking from experience here.)

4 **Take care when participating in any type of ritual with your immortal.** If he asks you to say a specific set of words in a language you don't understand, (gently) refuse. You might find yourself married to him, or even enslaved to him. Or worse, vowing to do something you don't want to do. And guess what? A human who breaks a vow to an immortal is no longer pre-dead—that human is just plain dead dead.

5 **Never ask him to make a promise to you.** Among the Demons and Angels especially, vows freely offered are utterly unbreakable. Those vows etch onto their flesh, black-ink branding them, weaving around their neck, shoulders and chest. If they fail to do as they've promised, those words grow, expand, and consume them, and then, once the ink covers them, their bodies harden into stone. They will forever suffer, trapped inside the indestructible shell, unable to get free. That happens, and their friends might come after you, vowing retribution.

6 **If you enjoy a cocktail on a date (and why not?) drink judiciously.** Do NOT let the liquor get the best of you. As an LG in the world of the undead, you have to be extra careful of your behavior—and excessive alcohol consumption is a slippery slope indeed. The last time I had a few too many on a date with a Demon, I ended up all over the Internet in a little production called *Angels Gone Wild*. Immortals can hold it better than you can . . . don't say I didn't warn you!

7 **And finally, if all doesn't go as swimmingly as you'd hoped—don't avoid his calls.** Not every Zombie is going to be your one-and-only. Maybe the chemistry just wasn't there, or you just don't like Death Metal music. You don't want to see him again—but he keeps calling. Sorry, ladies, but you are going to have to be forthright about it. KIND, if you value your extremities—but honest. With his sense of smell, he'll track you down no matter where you hide, so do yourself a favor and let him down firmly but gently. And if you think Zombie George might be totally right for one of your girlfriends, by all means hook a BLGF up! If you're lucky, he'll set you up with one of *his* friends—the one who prefers Lynyrd Skynyrd.

Friends, as always, I hope this helps you navigate life in the freak lane. Next month, we'll attack such ticklish topics as inviting his pack to dinner and running into his ex at a party. Meanwhile . . . don't do anything that I wouldn't do! (And you know what an Angel I am.) ❖

Beauty Secrets

You Can't Afford to Miss

Look Eternally Fresh All Day, Even When You're Howling the Night Away—and Keep Your Creature in Tip-Top Shape, Too!

Davyd Shay *is a renowned Holly-wood makeup artist (and judging from the hours he keeps, possibly an immortal himself) who never powders and tells, but loves to give advice. To him, a gorgeous LG is an informed LG. Because, let's face it, dating an immortal can be thrilling, but it also has a downside. Here are a few pointers for tackling the less glamorous side of being glamorous: nuts-and-bolts answers to your most often-asked questions.*

Q. I'm dating a Werewolf—great guy, hot as hell, amazing kisser when he actually gets the stubble off his face—but between you and me, sometimes he smells a little like . . . wet dog. There, I said it! What can I do? I adore the guy, but that odor is killing me!

A. No one likes a stink fest. So, if you don't have the heart to tell him it's time for a hose-down, start out your night together with a shared shower and a good lathering with one of the gels or body shampoos from the WereSkin line. They're specifically formulated to leave him smelling great while maintaining a soft, silky coat. (WereSkin also makes a fantastic shave and soothe kit, and if he uses it properly, you'll never have to worry about pesky stubble burn again!) And don't worry, these products improve the health of human skin and hair, too, and won't cause you to grow a beard or braid-able leg hair, as rumor would have you believe. If he likes the product, send him home with a gift basket of the stuff. Or if you want to play it a little more subtly, leave it in his shower the next time you spend the night at his place.

Q. I know Demons love eyes. In fact, I hear it's possible for an LG to hypnotize a Demon with her eyes if she can keep his attention long enough. How can I make the most of mine, attract one of these hellish hotties for myself, and do a little hypnotizing of my own?

A. Take some tips from other cultures: liner, liner, liner! Kohl or black eyeliner has been a standard cosmetic since Cleopatra's time, and remains so to this day. Why? Because it's sultry, seductive, and lets your Demon know you're ready to explore your wild side without you ever having to say a word.

If you're really ready to live on the edge, try the new Nightshade Drops from G'Oreal. The effect is only temporary, and they shouldn't be used more than once a week, but just a drop in each eye will give you luminous whites while enhancing the natural color of your irises. After just one application, looking away from you won't be an option for the drop-dead Demon you lock eyes with.

Q. I've heard about this Perle Dust stuff for Angels. Is it safe for me to use on my own skin? Can I use it like body glitter? And if so, will it actually attract other immortals or repel them?

A. Perle Dust is one of the Angelic world's best-kept secrets! Not only does it provide wings with an iridescent luster, it has a soft, sweet aroma that somehow soothes the worst of moods for many of the species. A little applied to your own skin will make you completely irresistible to any Angel nearby, as well it serves as walking Prozac to humans, Vamps, and Weres.

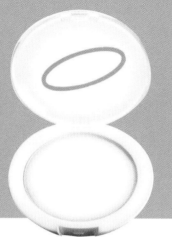

With that in mind, use it with caution. Apply it too liberally and you might just find every Demon in the area snarling at you. (The dust actually worsens their moods.) The effect on Zombies is the same as that of Sanding Sugar: Zombie Boy will be flooded with a need to taste you. He could lose control and you could lose a limb. Be cautious and sprinkle lightly.

Q. My Vampire boyfriend is a rock star in the bedroom, but he tends to leave . . . love bites on my neck. I'm not ready to reveal him to my co-workers but I think they're starting to suspect. How can I cover those marks up? I can't wear a turtleneck—I live in Miami!

A. Love bites are a definite "side effect" of doing the horizontal mambo with the undead, but when the sex is that hot, it's hard to care until the sun comes up. One of the best products on the market right now for covering those telltale marks is RecoverGirl's Queen of the Night concealer. It's specially formulated to hide those betraying Vampire bites. Thank heavens for modern cosmetic technology!

That stuff can be pricey, though, so if you're on a budget and in need of an instant fix, there is something else you can try—if your Vampire guy is willing, that is. You need a little of his blood, so ask nicely and be sure he knows it's for your skin. Just pat it on the same way you would concealer and presto! Bye-bye love bites. You'll swear it's magic, and come to think of it, I guess it is! Trust me when I say the Countess of Bathory was onto something with her virgin blood baths. Oh, no, I didn't! Oh, yes, I did!

Some Final Words of Advice . . . Take care of yourselves, darlings. I like to say that if you don't take care of yourself, no one else will want to (immortals included). That means inside and out. Watch your diet, drink plenty of water (and not too many Angeltinis or Dirty Devils), and remember: Beauty really isn't skin deep, it starts in the soul! If you're in love with an immortal, you want that beauty to last for a long, long time. So be happy, smile, live, and love well. It will shine through on your face and keep you looking beautiful for many years (and maybe even centuries) to come! ❖

Heartburn "Dragon" You Down?

That Dragon you're dating is flaming hot and so are his tastes—and that can be tough on your tender tummy. For him, there's no such thing as too much Tabasco or too many nights at the all-you-can-inhale Indian buffet...but if too much spice has you breathing flames hotter than his, you need Pepto Dismal. One swallow will quench the fire in your belly and ignite the one in your heart!

If you can't take the heat, take Pepto Dismal!

Lotions and Potions and Scrubs— *Oh, My!*

> Skin, hair, and body taking an immortal beating? We've got killer spa recipes you can replicate at home to restore that Angel-fresh glow from follicle to toe!

As much as we love them, our undead mates can be hard on our delicate complexions, muscles, and even our hair. In the heat of the moment, fangs can graze, talons can scratch—and oh, that abrasive fur stubble! Scales can turn even an innocent make-out session into a trip to the medicine cabinet for first-aid cream. And a sexy midnight romp under a full moon insures an achy back and sore feet the next day. What's an LG to do?

We all cherish a day of pampering at the local spa—but that can be a pricey and time-consuming affair for those of us who work hard by day and play hard by night. With these luscious preparations—designed especially for your creature-ravaged features—you can create your own rejuvenating spa experience at home and heal what ails you, whether you run with the Wolves or dance with the Vampires.

Unzombifying Zesty Lemon-Orange Bath

After a weekend of relaxation with your Zombie, you may be feeling a little bit lethargic—a little too mellow to face the world with your usual vim and vigor. No problem! To regain the bounce in your step and the gleam in your eye, try a splashy soak in this stimulating and revitalizing aromatherapy bath mixture.

Draw a warm (but not too hot) bath and add:

¼ cup grated lemon peel (for lethargy)

¼ cup grated orange peel (to combat anxiety)

1 tablespoon dried parsley (for stimulation)

1 tablespoon dried comfrey (a mild antiseptic)

A handful of crushed Doritos (to remind you of him!)

Put on your favorite upbeat music, sink into the tub, and breathe deeply, inhaling through your nose and exhaling through your mouth. The combination of fruits, herbs, and nacho cheese will bring you back to your bouncy self in no time!

Oatmeal, Avocado, and Dragon-Scale Body Scrub

Scales are for Dragons, not for delicate LGs . . . so calm down that irritated, creature-scraped skin with this soothing exfoliator that includes real ground Dragon scales. (Collect them from the bedsheets or the next time you give him a rubdown.) For best results, apply this with a muslin "mitt" you can make yourself.

½ cup blue or silver Dragon scales (or substitute dry-roasted almonds)

1 cup dry oatmeal

1 ripe avocado

Grind the scales (or almonds) in a blender or coffee grinder until medium-fine. Add the oatmeal and place the dry mixture into a muslin bag large enough to fit your hand into.

Halve the avocado, remove the pit, and scoop out the meat into a bowl. Mash until creamy.

Using your "mitt" full of the dry mixture, spread the avocado over your body, concentrating on areas that are particularly rough and scaly. Rub vigorously, in circular motions, so that the roughness of the scales or almonds exfoliates as the avocado smoothes and moisturizes. After ten minutes, rinse with warm water and pat dry.

NOTE: If there are Zombies in your life, make sure you are in a locked room when indulging in this treatment, as they are notoriously fond of guacamole.

Monstrously Moist Body Butter

Dry, rough skin is the bane of all LGs—especially those of us engaged in close encounters of the immortal kind. This ultra-soothing concoction will cure what ails you, from flame-singe to neck abrasion to that pesky fur burn.

2 tablespoons grated beeswax

1 teaspoon Wolfbane Ale (or substitute any light-colored beer)

1 teaspoon distilled water

½ cup cocoa butter

1 tablespoon sesame oil

1 tablespoon coconut oil

1 tablespoon olive oil

In a double boiler, melt the beeswax, beer, and water together over a low flame. Spoon in the cocoa butter and blend. Stirring constantly, gradually blend in the remaining ingredients. Pour into a glass jar (the mixture will thicken as it cools). Apply liberally wherever you are feeling dry, scratchy, or uncomfortable.

Demon-Fighting Foot Scrub

If you torture your feet in stilettos all day, then romp around the ritual pyre at night, your LG feet might be starting to resemble those Demon hooves of his! Smooth away your calluses, blisters, and bruises with this bracing scrub—best when applied with a sacred Demon stone.

½ cup dry cornmeal

2 tablespoons avocado oil

1 Demon Stone (If you can't wait until he's away from home to steal one of these hellish rocks that all Demon's keep under their beds to ward away sweet dreams, use a pumice stone, found in any drug or cosmetics store.)

Mix the cornmeal and avocado oil. Spread on achy and unsightly feet and rub in thoroughly with the Demon or pumice stone, concentrating on heels and callused areas. Rinse with warm water, pat dry—and you're ready to romp!

Angel-Sweet Lip Potion

Do I need to tell you that your lips deserve as much attention as the rest of your tormented skin and body? After all, they are bearing the brunt of those delicious kisses, as well as the frigid breezes at his heavenly hideaway. But use it with caution when in "mixed company." Both Zombies and Weres have been known to get a little bit bitey when stimulated by the scent, and you don't want to lose those pretty lips altogether!

3 teaspoons grated beeswax

5 teaspoons cosmetic-grade jojoba oil

1 teaspoon honey

1 teaspoon sugar

1 teaspoon Perle Dust for sparkle (or use baking powder)

Melt the wax and oil in a double boiler over a low flame (or use the microwave on 50 percent power for approximately 1 minute). Blend in the honey, sugar, and Perle Dust or baking powder. Pour the mixture into a small jar and let cool until thickened. Smooth over dry or cracked lips and then call your Angel over for a taste test!

And just in case your tastes run in a different vein—here are a few variations:

- To drive your **Demon** wild, add a drop of coconut essential oil when you add the honey to give him that taste of the paradise he's lost.
- **Vamps** like nothing better than bright red lips! To remind him of his favorite snack, add a bit of your favorite red lipstick when you melt the wax and oil, and mix thoroughly.
- **Weres** love the scent of the outdoors, and that calls for a drop of mint essential oil (spearmint or peppermint). One taste and he'll be panting for more.
- **Dragons** get off on anything spicy, so cinnamon is a must. During the melting process, stir your balm with a cinnamon stick and vavoom!
- **Zombies** make no secret of the fact that they're plagued by chapped lips of their own, so add a touch of dew to your kiss with cosmetic-grade aloe gel after the melting process for kisses that'll soothe you both.
- And finally, even **Angels** need a break from all things sweet and sugary. Surprise him by adding a touch of tangy citrus essential oil to your balm (lemon or grapefruit work well) when adding the honey. ❖

Your immortal soulmate is out there . . . and we can help you find him.

Tired of looking for an Angel but going home with a Demon? Ready to bed the undead but not sure where to find the Zombie that's right for you? Your happy ending may be just a few clicks away—at **mythmatch.com**.

Fill out our simple questionnaire and tap into our enormous database of immortals looking for love with the perfect LG. You could be lovebit by Valentine's Day or branded by your birthday!

mythmatch.com

Why, Oh Why, Do We Love THEM So?

Nine Reasons We Crave Immortals

What is it about undead dudes that really gets us going? Their looks, for sure—whether your taste runs to sensitive Angel types or steamin' Demons. But there are so many other reasons to fall for an immortal, and we've assembled our Top 9—you can decide the 10th!

1. Their manly beauty doesn't have an expiration date, and neither does their dangerous bad-boy appeal! He'll look just as handsome—and still have new tricks up his flowing sleeve—for all eternity. So . . . go ahead, Dragon-lover, play with fire every day—those flames will never die. And he'll never have to go on your insurance plan, either.

2. You'll never be ashamed to be seen with him. Most immortals dress better than we do (though some can use a little help from us . . . if he's one of them, see page 67 for helpful tips on making over his wardrobe). So, say goodbye to phrases like, "You're not going to wear that, are you?" and walk down the street proudly beside him. (You might even want to borrow some of his scarves—especially if you are hiding a few telltale "love bites.")

3. They can afford to show you a good time. Living forever is great for the bank account—they've been stashing away dough since the days of pirate treasure, and they know the stock market like the backs of their hairy hands. Go ahead and buy the strappy sandals and the red patent pumps—your howlin' hottie won't complain when the bill comes.

4. Due to circumstances beyond their control, very few immortals have mothers. Think about it. This means you'll never have a mother-in-law to pass judgment on how you dress, cook, or keep house. You heard right: there's no such thing as a "monster-in-law."

5. Enjoy flying? How about without a plane? Yep, you're bound to get carried away when you date an immortal—and I mean dinner for two in Paris followed by a stroll around Sydney harbor. No need to fasten your seatbelts, either. These guys have a perfect safety record, even when carrying a dressed-to-the-nines LG under their ever-lovin' wings.

6. Hard-bodied perfection is the norm among immortals. Who knows why, but those rippling muscles and washboard abs go with the territory. No matter how many bags of Doritos your Zombie scarfs down or how much steak tartare your Werewolf devours, he'll maintain his glorious physique for the duration. (And, with the workout he gives you, so will you!) Oh, and as for his dome—he'll never go bald, guaranteed.

7. Chores no more. Not only are immortals eager to please, most of them never sleep. So go ahead, lazybones, stay in bed til three. Just leave him a to-do list and your house will be spotless and your fridge filled with your favorite treats by the time you get up.

8. Not just sexy—romantic, too. What might seem old-fashioned to some guys is "classic" to an immortal, from bringing home flowers to remembering every anniversary (including the first bite or first full moon together). After all, he was once a genuine Victorian gentleman. If rose petals on the sheets never get old for you, go immortal!

9. Need space? No problem. An immortal is never clingy or (too) possessive—on the contrary, he is happy to let you enjoy a night out with the gals or watch *Twilight* for the 25th time. Maybe it's because he needs his alone time too, to enjoy a wing massage, moisturize his paws, oil his scales, or (in Zombie's case) reach that last level of his favorite video game. You'll never feel smothered—except occasionally by his awesome wings, but that's okay, right? ❖

COUPLE CRAVINGS QUIZ

Do you have what it takes to date a creature of "myth?"

Dating a live guy is tough enough, but when the man you're crushing on sports the immortal tag, an LG has to be quick on her feet and open to anything. Take our quiz to see if you're on the highway to heaven or a road trip to hell.

1. When you realize the hot, sexy Vampire next to you is staring at your neck, you . . .

a. Flip your hair over your shoulder to give him a better look at your pulse. He can look, but he can't have! (2 points)

b. Leave the room as fast as you can. You're willing to share a juice box with him—you're just not willing to *be* the juice box. (1 point)

c. Walk right up to him, lay your hands flat on his chest, and whisper seductively into his ear, "Find me later, and we'll play a little game of Bite the Apple." (3 points)

2. While making out with your Werewolf boyfriend for the first time, you catch a glimpse of his sharp, deadly claws. You . . .

a. Run. The last time you saw nails like that you were watching a horror movie, and you haven't forgotten what happened to that stupid girl who stuck around! (1 point)

b. Stay put. You're scared, but you're willing to give him a chance to prove just how quickly his inner animal can be tamed! (2 points)

c. Shiver and kiss him again. Who cares about a few potential scratches? Actually, you crave those scratches because really, those muscles of his are to die for (literally). And besides, there's no reason to worry about that annoying bra clasp now. (3 points)

3. On your first date with Zombie Boy, he takes you to the grocery store. The plan? To run through the aisles tossing whatever looks good into the basket—then go home and have a junk food orgy. You . . .

a. Ditch him while he's entranced by the Doritos. Your idea of spontaneous fun is showing up at a restaurant without a reservation. This behavior is just . . . odd. (1 point)

b. Play along. After loading your bounty into the car, you suggest a quiet spot overlooking the town to enjoy your goodies, instead of heading home to the couch. Who knows? Maybe he's right and Twinkies *are* best eaten four at a time. (3 points)

c. Smile and go along for the ride, all the while hoping none of your friends see you acting like a lunatic. And did he just rip open that Ding Dong package with his teeth? (2 points)

4. On your one-week anniversary with a Demon, you plan a romantic evening at home but he says he'd prefer a wild night clubbing. You are very . . .

a. Excited. That's what you really wanted to do, anyway. Throwing back a few cold ones and grinding together till dawn always revs your engine. (3 points)

b. Angry. You did not want to spend such a special night surrounded by writhing, sweating bodies. You wanted to spend the night with only one writhing, sweating body: his. (1 point)

c. Unsure, but willing to compromise. After all, you love watching this party animal in action, and at the end of the night he's bound to have some excess energy you can channel into a different kind of action. (2 points)

5. You've been dating an Angel for several months, but you still haven't gotten him into bed. You . . .

a. Strip in front of him and ask him to show you how "good" he can be. (1 point)

b. Sit down and have a heart to heart with him about your needs. You know there's nothing he loves more than talking about feelings. (3 points)

c. Remind yourself that this particular guy has been around since almost the beginning of time, and a few months to him is like the blink of an eye. Continue to wait for him to make his move. You don't want to scare him away. (2 points)

6. You've touched your Dragon date without permission—a big-time no-no. He whisks you away to his lair, planning to make you his love slave. You . . .

a. Play along. "Love slave" is your favorite bedroom game. But next time, he has to wear the chains. (2 points)

b. Apologize grudgingly, then ask why the hell he's so cranky, anyway. His gaze has been caressing your body all night long, and you weren't giving him the verbal hand-slap, now were you? (3 points)

c. Fear for your life and reach for your cell phone to dial 9-1-1 as quickly as possible. (1 point)

7. You've been dating your Dragon for an entire month now (yes, you survived the mandatory stay in his lair) but you haven't yet kissed each other good night. You are apprehensive because his mouth may be too hot to handle! Tongue blisters, anyone? You're frustrated and desperate, so you . . .

a. Forget the kiss and decide to take sexual matters into your own hands. Literally. Both of you end up satisfied. (3 points)

b. Break up with him. You're both highly sexual creatures and you just can't deal with the lack of intimacy anymore. No matter how sexalicious he is, you've been having more fun by yourself! (1 point)

c. Continue on the way things are. You're falling in love with him, and you don't want to mess it up, even if you *are* practically living in a cold shower. Your new goal? Research ways to fix the problem. (2 points)

8. That hot Demon guy of yours suggests a quick stop for a little late night Ritual of the Wine. You . . .

a. Grab your favorite Zinfandel. As long as there are some wine rites happening, why not include yours? (2 points)

b. Reach for the closest cross and bottle of Holy Water. (1 point)

c. Hop on the Internet so you can research every aspect of the ceremony, including where you stand, what you say, and what shoes are most appropriate. (3 points)

9. The Angel you hope to date admits he's not sure if he's naughty enough to fully fall for you. You . . .

a. Are horrified that you even considered stealing an Angel from heaven and point him skyward. Stat! (1 point)

b. Are convinced that this is the guy for you. Now's the time to surprise him with your "emergency kit" containing crotchless panties, handcuffs with the missing key, candles, and a bottle of Karo syrup. (3 points)

c. Let him know you're there for him, whatever his decision. (2 points)

10. The thought of living forever with your immortal lover is . . .

a. Kick ass. 'Nuff said. (3 points)

b. Horrifying! Sure, you'll be gorgeous for eternity, but enough is enough. How many times can you pick his underwear up off the floor before you start praying for death? (1 point)

c. Terrifying, yet exciting. You'll learn everything there is to know about each other and have eternity to share everything. But in the end will you like what you learn and share? (2 points)

SCORING

If you scored **10–16 points,** you should stick to dating human men. Immortals just aren't for you. Their otherworldly traits tend to freak you out, and the thought of dealing with the same man for eternity leaves you cold. So, if ever you're tempted to experiment with someone outside your species, just remember that when they say, "We're forever," they mean it literally.

If you scored **17–23 points**, you straddle the "Should I or Shouldn't I?" fence, and that isn't good for you or your immortal. You need to have a serious heart to heart with yourself before settling in for a long-term—*really* long-term—otherworldly relationship. Is he worth dying for? Is an eternity with him better than a human lifetime without him? If you aren't careful, your immortal will make the decision for you—and you may not like the results.

If you scored **24–30 points,** you are ready, willing, and eager to date a creature of the otherworld. Your immortal's differences excite and tantalize you, and no matter what happens, you're in this for the long haul. Just like he is. ❖

Wine This Fine...Takes an Eternity.

At Gallows, the finest grapes, grown in the unparalleled Carpathian region, are lovingly harvested, blended, aged, and bottled (all after nightfall) by our legion of undead vintners–devoted professionals who have honed their wine-making skills over thousands of years.

The only Vampire-owned and operated winery in the world, Gallows is especially proud of its rich, blood-red Cabernets, Pinots, and Merlots, all guaranteed to satisfy even the most discerning palate.

"We like to say that opening a bottle of Gallows is like opening a vein–it's that good," says founder Julio Gallows. We think you'll agree.

E&J Gallows Wines

Laws of Attraction

Species-by-Species Secrets for Making Him Your Otherworldly One-and-Only

There's nothing wrong with giving fate a nudge . . . sometimes that bitch can be way too slow! Here are a few of our quickest and naughtiest tricks to attract an otherworldly boyfriend, whether your taste runs to elusive Vamps, woolly Weres, or adorable Angels.

If you want to date a
VAMPIRE

• Prick your finger and dab a tiny bead of blood on each of your pulse points, the same way you would dab perfume. Make sure you hit all of your erogenous zones! With every beat of your heart, the delicious scent of your blood will tantalize his senses.

• Sign up as a volunteer at your local Vamp Camp, where older Vampires teach younger ones how to survive. You'll be nibbled on repeatedly, and as they say, sometimes a single taste is all an addiction requires.

• Wear the sexiest vintage gown you can find, preferably something off the shoulder, and pin up your hair. This will remind him of his younger days, when his hormones were out of control, as well as put the focus on your neck, making it impossible for him to look away. And, of course, make sure to accidentally bump into him so he gets the best possible scent and view.

If you want to date a
WEREWOLF

• Remember Little Red Riding Hood? Well, she knew her wolves. The next time you're going to see your Were, don a bright red cape with nothing underneath. His inner animal will go wild.

• Wolves love the chase. Ditch the sweats and don that sexy sports bra and matching too-tight shorts, then take your morning jog through the woods. When you hear him howling, answer back with a sultry, "Catch me if you can!"

• Werewolves were born to take orders from an Alpha (unless yours *is* the Alpha, of course, then it's a whole other game), so don't be afraid to be firm with him. "Sit" and "stay" work remarkably well, and so do "kiss me" and "up, boy." The Alpha will resist and offer commands of his own. Obeying is up to you.

If you want to date a
DRAGON

- These white-hot boys once feasted on virgins, so give him a taste of what he's been missing—chain yourself to his bed and make yourself an oh-so-willing sacrifice.

- Forget borrowing a cup of sugar. Your excuse for stopping by? You've run out of matches and need his help lighting your fire.

- Tell him all about your intense fear of flying. There's a very good chance he'll offer to help you overcome it by taking you where you need to go—safely on his back. At the very least, you'll earn a few frequent-flyer miles as he escorts you around town in an effort to ease your fears! And while you're up there, ask him where he wants you to keep your hands . . .

If you want to date a
ZOMBIE

• Carry a sweet treat in your purse at all times. His sense of smell is highly attuned, and once he catches a whiff of your dessert, he'll follow you wherever you go! You might even get a little nibbling out of the deal.

• Get your mosh on and drag him to the local punk club. When peeled off their couches, Zombies love loud music and raucous crowds. Afterward, getting your Zombie to go horizontal will be easy!

• Forgo the floral-scented lotion and apply something edible behind your ears, then deliver his "dinner" to his door. He'll forget all about the video games he's been playing for the past three days.

If you want to date an
ANGEL

• These sexy wingers can't resist a damsel in distress. So, the next time you're feeling blue, head out and get your cry on (while wearing a white corset and stockings). Soon you'll be wrapped in soft white wings and strong, muscled arms.

• Skydive in your underwear and mindtreat him by thinking of something super-sexy while airborne. You'll catch his eye as he's passing, and no matter how pure his heart, he won't be able to resist following you down.

• Transform your rosary into your favorite fashion flair. Nothing says *I'm a good girl looking for a little Angelic loving* like Vatican-approved accessorizing!

If you want to date a
DEMON

• Break out the Tabasco sauce. Demons love all things spicy, so seeking out scorching new dishes to try will show him you mean business. Pretty soon you'll be the only scorching new dish on his menu.

• Horns are sensitive. When you get your digits on his, treat them the way you'd treat any other sensitive part of his body, and soon you'll have him purring like a fork-tongued kitten. And yes, the bigger the horns, the bigger the . . . you know. (WARNING: Before attempting to handle horns, find out if his ivory head-towers produce a toxin that could kill you. Smart LGs know how to play it safe, and horn condoms come in a variety of textures and tastes.)

• Walk up to your hell-tastic crush, and whisper these four little words: *You. Me. Reverse Cowgirl.* You'll be burning up the sheets in no time. ❖

Heaven is closer than you think!

You love your Angel's heavenly glow….
Now you can have it for yourself with
Perle Dust—the Angels' best-kept secret
for divinely dewy skin from wing-tip to toe.
Smoothe it on after every shower to stay
eternally youthful and feather-soft.
You'll make him fall all over again!

Perle Dust

A Kiss Is NOT Just a Kiss

Immortals We Crave Divulge Their Lip-Smacking Turn-Ons

When it comes to kissing an immortal, the myth-information is rampant. A Vampire will fall into a blood rage if your gums are cut. Wrong. A Were will leave fur in your mouth. Nope. A Dragon will blister your throat. Hardly. A Zombie will chew your tongue off. Maybe. An Angel won't open his mouth. Come on! That one is flat out ridiculous. And a Demon will suck out your soul. Only if you're lucky!

So, what's fact and what's fiction? And what do these undead guys really like best, anyway? We asked some of our favorite immortals to describe the hot smooching they crave—so get ready for the ultimate kiss and tell . . . .

Zombie Carl: The best kiss is the one shared while eating. Grab a bite of something tempting between your teeth, dangle it in front of me, and I'll meet you more than halfway. And don't be afraid to tell me if I chomp on something I shouldn't.

Demon Markov: The best kiss is the one that works its way right down to your . . . lap. I like my woman to wear lipstick—preferably a soft, innocent pink. The more rings she leaves behind, the better the time I had.

Angel Joseph: Because I can read a woman's mind, it's better for both of us if she clears her thoughts. If she starts mentally critiquing my performance, I'm outta there.

Werewolf Drew: In a word—chase. When I hunt and run my woman down, the victory kiss is explosive. Both of our hearts are racing, and our bodies are in tune and totally primed. I'm even willing to let her break away just so I can track her again.

Vampire Evgeny: I know it's old-fashioned (hey, I'm an old-fashioned guy), but seeing a woman tug her lips with her teeth makes me want to kiss them (and take a little nibble while I'm at it).

Angel Michael: A nice romantic comedy always gets me in the mood for a little lip lock. A fave? *Date with an Angel*, of course.

Dragon Richard: I'd been working with a very hot chick on a new design for a plane based on Dragon flight. I spent weeks fulfilling her every request . . . unfortunately all work related, although there were definitely sparks between us. One night, while running tests, I took a shot and casually mentioned she could touch me if she wanted to. She touched me, all right! Light at first, starting up top, but then she grew bolder—and moved lower. I loved it! By the time she reached my navel, I had to grab her up so we could kiss. Truth be told, I almost set the blueprints on fire. So if you couldn't guess, my favorite kisses are the ones that come with a LOT of skin-on-skin action. I've been with her ever since.

Vampire Paul: When I taste blood while I'm kissing a woman, yeah, that gets me really excited. And, though it puts her in danger of being thrown across the bed and ravaged, not to worry—she'll never be drained. We do have some restraint, after all.

Zombie Brandon: One night, my girlfriend said she wanted to pop something into the DVD player. Next thing you know, her beautiful face appeared on screen, and she was telling me exactly how she wanted me to kiss her. And where. That night we wore out the pause button trying out each suggestion. She's my new favorite show!

Demon Parton: If you want to taste these lips, never take me to see a romantic comedy. There's not many things as close to hell, in my opinion. Now a good festival of *Saw* movies—that might get my blood flowing to all the right places. . . .

continued

Vampire Craig: Nibbling is what really starts me up. I can't tell you how sexy it is for a woman to nibble on me. The first girlfriend I had after my change was a little nervous about the whole biting thing, so she said she'd go first. She nibbled my ears, the tips of my fingers, down my neck. She got me so hot, I couldn't even think about a feeding.

Dragon Jason: My skin is super-sensitive after I shift from my Dragon form, and if I'm already "in the mood," touching really stokes my internal furnace. But kissing me? On my mouth, my neck, my chest, my . . . anywhere—it's like my whole focus narrows down to that point of contact. When I get hyper-focused like that, I can drive a woman out of her mind with pleasure. Consider yourself warned.

Angel Gabe: I tend to know what's best. Always. (And before some Demon makes a wisecrack, remember that it's not bragging if it's true.) I also know when disaster is on its way. So don't be afraid to slap a blindfold around my eyes and put stoppers in my ears—then overwhelm my sense of taste with you. That's one sure way to help me sit back, forget what's coming, and enjoy the ride.

Werewolf Travis: I'd been out with this girl a few times, but nothing had happened yet, and I was beginning to think she wasn't interested. A full moon was approaching, so I was trying to get her comfortable with the idea of being with me—in any form. But no matter what I did to relax her, she gave me no clues about how she would react to my change. Then, one night, she leaned up against the wall, licked her lips, and asked if I wanted to kiss her. All my blood went south, so I could only nod. Just before I could plant one on her, she said she didn't like to share, and that if I were hers, I'd have to mark my territory with my mouth. That was language I could understand, and I knew she'd accept me, no matter what shape I took. That increased my excitement more than anything else, and we ended up sharing the sexiest damn kiss of my life. When we parted, we were both branded.

Demon Nathan: If there's a rule, I want to break it. Maybe because I hate the fact that any vow a Demon makes is etched into his (smokin' hot) bod and when he breaks *that* . . . well . . . it's game over. My girlfriend knows me better than I realized and came up with all sorts of guidelines and precepts of what we could and couldn't do. No kissing in the morning, no kissing until the third date . . . on and on it went. I had the best time thrashing every single one of them. And the only consequence? Her moans of pleasure.

Zombie Jack: Hey, I'm just thrilled she's thinking about kissing me at all. Most girls are scared to even be near me, thinking I'm planning to saw open their noggin and suck up their brains like spaghetti noodles or something. But if she really wants to rev my engine, she needs to wear edible panties. 'Nuff said, right? ❖

Because you need to know the whole story.

There are lots of products on the market that can tell you if you're pregnant—but only U.P.T. is specially designed to tell you who (or what) the father is…without the hassle or expense of doctors and blood tests. In just five minutes, the little window on the U.P.T. stick will indicate "**V**" for Vampire, "**D**" for Demon, "**A**" for Angel, "**Z**" for Zombie, or "**W**" for Werewolf—taking the guesswork and concern out of the most exciting day of your life!

u·p·t

UNDEAD PREGNANCY TEST

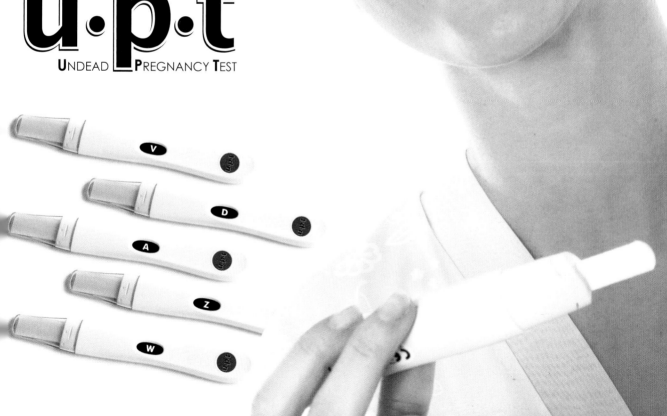

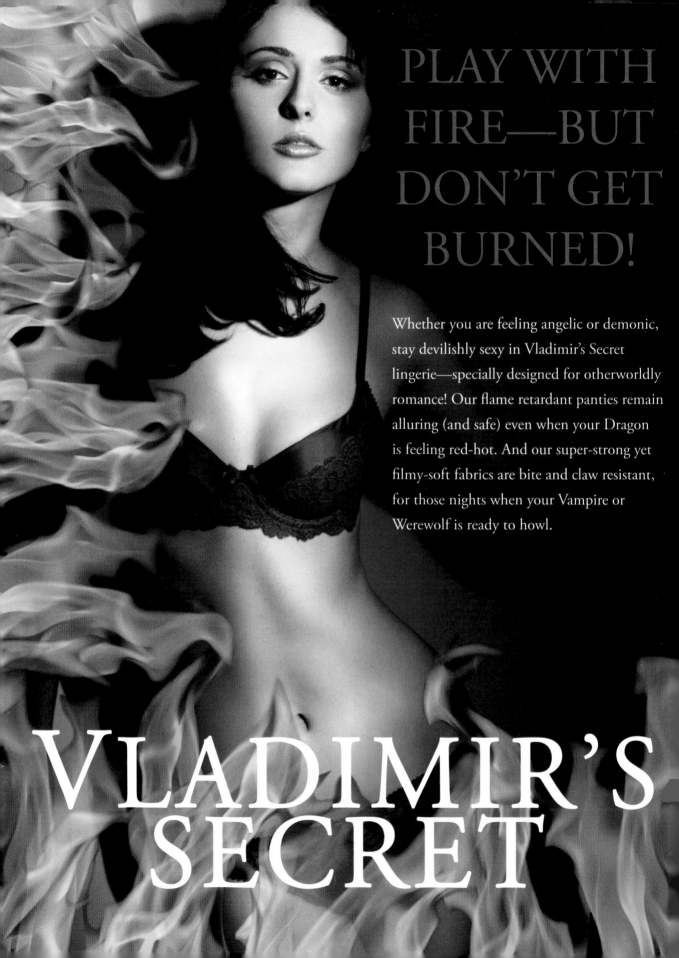

PLAY WITH FIRE—BUT DON'T GET BURNED!

Whether you are feeling angelic or demonic, stay devilishly sexy in Vladimir's Secret lingerie—specially designed for otherworldly romance! Our flame retardant panties remain alluring (and safe) even when your Dragon is feeling red-hot. And our super-strong yet filmy-soft fabrics are bite and claw resistant, for those nights when your Vampire or Werewolf is ready to howl.

VLADIMIR'S SECRET

When the Other Woman Is Immortal

Want to Make Sure He Only Has Fangs for YOU? Start by Knowing the Enemy!

Dating an immortal is thrilling, but you have to be tough (and I'm not referring to your pain threshold here). Other ladies are bound to come sniffing around that sexy creature of yours—some of them literally. You might know the ropes when it comes to fending off other LGs, but if you want to prevail against those bodacious otherworldly babes making eyes at your guy, you have to understand them. Here's the skinny on how he interacts with women of his own kind, and how you can win in the battle of the species and hold onto his heart (not literally).

VAMPIRES

A female Vampire can't offer her mate a delicious meal straight from her vein because, despite what you may have heard, Vamp blood is unappetizing to other Vampires. She can, however, match his unnatural strength—making for some wild and crazy sex play. He knows she won't break when he touches her, and that means he doesn't have to worry about losing control in the bedroom (or kitchen, or coffin). Since you can't match her superhuman strength, you've got to show him that holding back, submitting, and switching roles can be just as exciting as throwing each other around with abandon.

So, if you're an LG with a fang fetish, let him know there can be strength in weakness—and wicked fun. Tie him up and prove who's boss. Sure, he could break through your fur-lined handcuffs if he really wanted to, but your playfully confident dominance will keep him in his place and loving it. Once you

are in charge of his pleasure, try giving him a taste of his own medicine by nibbling on *his* neck for change. Or make him lick you all over without once baring his fangs. He does, and he'll have to be punished. By the time you're done, he'll know there's no other girl for him.

NO-NOs: Never draw your own blood in an attempt to lure a Vampire into drinking from you. They have rules they "live" by, and this goes against an important one. Just so you are clear on your guy's code:

Rule One: Never drink from an unwilling human.

Rule Two: Never drink more than a pint from a single donor, unless you are performing a transformation.

Rule Three: Never drink from a living source in public.

Rule Four: Never drink and fly.

WEREWOLVES

A female wolf has the same animal instincts as her male counterpart, which means her sex drive is off the charts—and that's attractive to guys of all varieties. Complicating matters further is the species' famous pack mentality, which might lead your Werewolf one-and-only to follow his buddies' lead, even when they are leading him into trouble. (If you ask him, "If your bwff Joey jumped into the sack with his girlfriend's sister, would you do the same?" The answer, sadly, is—probably. Unless, of course, your wolf has permanently marked you as his. Then he's all yours, too, and there's nothing to worry about on that score.)

So . . . if you are dating a Werewolf, you have to be willing to embrace your adventurous spirit and unleash the animal lurking inside you. Show him that you are game for anything, from camping in the woods during a full moon to having sex in the bathroom during your parents' anniversary party. And what about his favorite fantasy game, Dog Chases Cat? Why not give it a try? Open yourself up to the paws-sibilities, and he'll never want to stray.

NO-NOs: Just because wolves run in packs doesn't mean you have the right to round up your own posse and invade his space. Territory is important to these four-legged sexpots, and if you venture into his lair uninvited, you may find your license to his body revoked.

DRAGONS

Because Dragons of both genders have such fierce tempers, their passion in the bedroom can be searing hot. Here's where the female Dragon has a bit of an advantage over you: her scaly exoskeleton makes her impervious to his fire, so no need for the asbestos lingerie. But with fiery natures come sizzling arguments, and that gets tiresome. Every guy needs a woman who knows how to cool him down, and that goes double for Dragons.

That's where the even-tempered LG comes in. Nurture your Dragon by picking your battles. Let him have his way sometimes, and he'll learn to let you have yours. Show him that a little bit of TLC can be as much of a turn-on as a tongue of flame. At the end of the day, he is sure to choose the LG goddess who soothes him over the Dragon babe with the built-in flame-thrower.

NO-NOs: Among Dragons, touching is considered a privilege, and permission must be granted before it is okay. Even a handshake or stroke of the backscales is unacceptable unless he makes the first move. So, until you've been given the go-ahead, keep your hands in your pockets or you might go home "red-handed" (or no-handed)!

One other thing: Never refer to your Dragon as a "hatchling," even if he is under 500 and doesn't look a day over 350. As cute as it sounds to human ears, the term is offensive. (How would you like it if he called you a fetus?)

ZOMBIES

Zombies are sweet, steady guys whose idea of a hot Saturday night is sitting on the couch next to their best girl, playing video games, and munching on food out of a bag. Women Zombies know this and don't try to change them. (Why would they? Zombie girls like to relax, too—and they know there's a lot to be said for a stay-at-home squeeze who is neither a party animal nor a workaholic with no time for love.)

Don't try to turn your Zombie into a Demon—appreciate him for who he is. (There's plenty of time for subtle renovations once he's yours for eternity.) Sit beside your couch potato and caress his thigh while he watches TV. Make him a delicious bowl of homemade salsa to go with his chips, and during a commercial, perform a little striptease just for him. He might even be so enthralled, he'll drop the remote and lunge for a little loving.

NO-NOs: You don't have to worry about rules or regulations when it comes to your Zombie—but these guys can be ultra sensitive about their flaws. Keep your criticism constructive and diplomatic. Instead of saying, "Why must you always toss bones under the coffee table?!" try, "Honey, I think it is sweet that you are leaving snacks for the cats—but since you ate our last kitten on Thursday, there's no need to do it anymore."

ANGELS

Angels, no matter their gender, have one thing in common: the desire to make the world a perfect place. While they do possess a deep capacity to love within their race, that love is usually so gentle it remains platonic—making it easier for you to compete with even the most radiant Angel girl. If Angels have a downside, it is that they tend to think they are always right. And, since they are keenly attuned to impending disaster, they are cautious by nature.

To keep your Angel under your spell, show him your mischievous side. As sweet as he is, he will enjoy learning that a bit of danger can be exciting—especially in the bedroom. Teach him a little game called "I've Been a Bad, Bad Girl," where you confess your "sins" and he punishes you for them. (Advise him that a good way to punish you is by making you fulfill all his heavenly fantasies!) Before you know it, he'll ditch his quest for world perfection and focus on perfecting your bliss!

NO-NOs: Try not to come on too strong with your gentle Angel. Instead, ease him into the sensual side of your relationship with long bubble baths and luscious wing massages accompanied by Gregorian chants and plenty of candles. You'll make him feel right at home, and that will help him open up to the sexy side of life. No man—not even one with God's cell phone number—can resist a woman who loves him for his virtues but inspires him to explore his vices.

DEMONS

Demons are the original hell-raisers and they live for the next good time. And once again, the females of this species can match their men's strength and party like rock stars. But excessive mayhem has its consequences—and excessive drinking and drugging is unlikely to lead to memorable sex (or any memory at all).

Don't worry that your Demon will find you boring if you don't match him pint for pint and party for party. Show him that remaining conscious and lucid has its advantages, too—especially in the bedroom. And there's nothing a Demon likes better than teaching a good girl to be bad, so take a deep breath and explore your own dark side a little. Think of some things you've always wanted to try but never had the nerve to, and ask him to help you get over your inhibitions. If the two of you can meet halfway, there'll be sparks galore.

NO-NOs: Expecting a commitment from a Demon is like expecting a Vampire to buy property on the sun—so have fun but guard your heart. It's not just girls who play with Dragons who risk getting burned. And be discreet. It is harder to repair a tarnished reputation than to get bloodstains out of a silk blouse. ❖

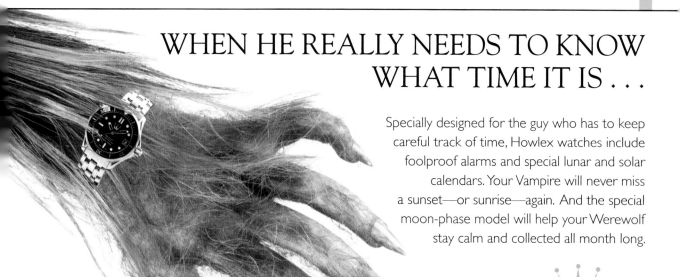

WHEN HE REALLY NEEDS TO KNOW
WHAT TIME IT IS . . .

Specially designed for the guy who has to keep careful track of time, Howlex watches include foolproof alarms and special lunar and solar calendars. Your Vampire will never miss a sunset—or sunrise—again. And the special moon-phase model will help your Werewolf stay calm and collected all month long.

HOWLEX

Ask Esmeralda
Straight Answers for Bitten Kittens, Wolf Bait, and Angel Cakes

Dr. Esmeralda Strong is both an AVC (American Vampire Council) and WIA (Worldwide Immortals Association) board-certified relationship therapist specializing in human and non-human couples counseling. She's appeared on numerous radio and television talk shows and is the author of the best-selling books, Bitten And Smitten—Now What? *and* Forbidden Fruit: Loving the Immortal Man.

Dear Dr. Strong,
I've been seeing the sexiest Vampire in town and our relationship is getting hot and heavy. He wants a taste, but I'm just not sure. What do you think? Should I let him bite me? I've never done this before!
Signed,
Virgin Veins

Dear Virgin,
I can guess what questions are rolling through your mind. Will the bite hurt? Good news is, it won't! Fangs produce a numbing agent. Will you scar? No again. A single lick of his tongue or a swipe of his blood when the sucking is over, and you'll heal right up. But here are two questions only your man can answer—questions you need to ask him before that first nibble, not after:

How often will he expect you to feed him?

Will you be his only living blood source?

Allowing your Vampire boyfriend to bite you is not a decision to be taken lightly. Sharing your blood is an intimate act, and the more he drinks, the more likely you are to bond to him mentally, physically, and sexually. Eventually, you'll reach a point where breaking that bond is impossible. Are you ready to take that step? Can you see yourself with him next month? Next year? Next decade?

As long as you both go into it with a full understanding of what it means for your relationship, then have at it! Consensual biting can be a very fulfilling experience.

• • •

Dear Dr. Strong,
I've been dating Mr. Wonder-Wolf for several months now, and things are getting serious between us. He's asked me to accept the mark of his pack so that I have their protection. Should I? What if we break up? Will all other wolves refuse to date me? What will my parents think?
Signed,
Hot for Hairy

Dear Hot,
Accepting a pack mark is definitely a serious step. If you plan on dating WonderWolf exclusively, then a pack mark is imperative. Weres can be especially territorial, and you don't want to run into a situation where a rival pack member decides to take what doesn't belong to him. In other words, YOU. War will erupt, and that's a fact.

So, here's what you need to know. There are two types of pack marks and I would assume your boyfriend is talking about the temporary one that disappears with each full moon (meaning you'll have to get it redone once a month). If that's the case, you'll only have to wait out the remaining days until the next full moon for the mark to disappear. And if you do break up after this mark fades, other wolves will indeed be able to date you.

As for the other kind of pack mark, it's permanent and is meant only for forever mates. It is traditionally applied as part of a sacred bonding ceremony. You should definitely ask him which mark he has in mind for you—because if you break up after receiving a permanent mark, no other wolf will ever be allowed to date you. (No humans, either.) Not without punishment. And with the wolves, punishment equals banishment or death. There are no other options.

Dear Dr. Strong,

My best friend is marrying a hunky Fire Demon and she's asked me to be the maid of honor for her destination wedding in Hawaii. My only problem? I'm dating an Ice Demon, and you know how those two breeds clash. I don't want to spend a weekend in Hawaii without my guy. What should I do?
Signed,
Ice, Ice Baby

Dear Ice,
You're right to be worried. The feud between Ice and Fire Demons began nearly a century ago as one of those typical male "I'm better than you/No, I'm better" things, and has only gotten worse since. However, I believe weddings fall under a special truce dispensation. Check with your local Demon council, a division of the WIA. Both parties might be required to sign an Abidance Contract for the duration of the wedding weekend, but I can't imagine either one would want to ruin what should be a very special event for you and the bride.

Don't be afraid to broach the subject of the contract, either. Being part of your friend's wedding is something you don't want to miss, so put your big girl panties on and deal with it. Once the contract is signed, you can forget your troubles and enjoy your time in the sun!

• • •

Dear Dr. Strong,

You might say I'm immortal-curious. I already know these guys are super-sexy because one of my LG bffs is dating a Vampire and another is dating a Zombie. I'd like to try a fallen Angel myself but have no clue where to start or how to find one. What should I do?
Signed,
Desperately Seeking Seduction

Dear Desperately,
Fallen Angels are a tough nut to crack—and I mean that almost literally. They've been kicked out of the heavens for being too naughty, but they aren't accepted in hell because they're still too nice. They are likely to have a Dr. Jekyll and Mr. Hyde thing going on, so you'll never know which side of the good-evil fence your immortal will be straddling on any given day. But if that's your thing, more power to ya. You can increase your chances of meeting a fallen Angel by spending time where they're likely to hang out. Here are two suggestions:

• Check out the Perpetual Calendar section on page 18—there you'll find highlights of the upcoming immortal gatherings including beach parties, balls, and council meetings.

• Because the fallen sometimes get their wings clipped before they're booted from the sky—it really depends on their level of naughtiness—they often miss flying. Try booking a trip to an exotic locale (check out "Thirteen Places to Go Before You Don't Die" on page 149). Maybe you'll luck out and sit next to your dream immortal!

• • •

Dear Dr. Strong,

I just broke up with my Zombie boyfriend and he won't leave me alone. I won't say things have reached the stalker level yet, but we've run into each other more times than can really be considered coincidence. He used to say he loved me for my brains and my body, but now I'm starting to think he meant that more literally than figuratively.
Signed,
Not Having It

Dear Not,
Zombies are the original obsessives—over video games, and sometimes over one particular woman. Just when you think you've evaded him, he'll pop up again. As exes go, this type can wear you out. Try talking to him. (Speak slowly as Zombies can be easily confused.) The problem may be as simple as the fact that he doesn't understand that you're no longer a couple. If straight talk doesn't work, you've got to play hardball. The next few times you go out, take a formidable male companion with you, mortal or immortal. Zombies understand territory and if he thinks you're now the mate of a more dominant male, he should back down, lose interest, and disappear.

If all else fails, use a bat. ❖

Tame your allergies—so you're ready to howl

Sniffles and sneezes putting a damper on romance? Show your allergies who's boss with Weretin, the over-the-counter medication formulated to subdue your sensitivity to a Werewolf's fur and dander. You'll be romping the night away with your beautiful beast in no time!

Non-Drowsy
Weretin
Weretin

Bloodstains On His Collar, Doritos In His Bed

Is your immortal just a little bit . . . immoral?

You don't want to go there, but you can't help it. You're suspicious that he's cheating. Immortals have lived a long time, and they know the tricks, so forget searching through texts or credit card receipts for proof of his infidelity. But even these canny supermen can't hide everything. As always, we're here to help—this time with a species-specific checklist of the signs that he might be straying. If you find yourself checking off more than two statements for your breed, it may be time to sit down and have a knee-to-groin chat with him.

If he's a Vampire:

❏ **1.** He says your bedposts look too much like stakes and he'd be more comfortable sleeping elsewhere.

❏ **2.** You hear him using your computer when he's supposed to be watching you sleep.

❏ **3.** He tries to talk you out of "converting" for him. "Eternity is a long time, you know . . ."

❏ **4.** He takes a long time to respond to your telepathic thoughts, and when he does, it's usually just a text message saying he's got bad reception.

❏ **5.** You find bloodstains on his collar, and they aren't yours. Plus, he hasn't nibbled your neck in weeks!

If he's a Werewolf:

❏ **1.** He tells you his skin is sensitive and he doesn't like to be scratched behind his ears anymore.

❏ **2.** He comes home with "cat hair" on his trousers—long, blond "cat hair."

❏ **3.** He says he has to be out late—on a night when there isn't a full moon—and that you shouldn't call him because he'll be busy in "meetings."

❏ **4.** He suddenly likes to take his long walks alone, though he never used to be the lone-wolf type.

❏ **5.** He constantly reminds you that wolves are pack animals and his friends need him more than you do.

If he's a Zombie:

❏ **1.** He claims he scratched his tongue on his dinner cow and can't lick you anymore.

❏ **2.** He says he can't meet your parents because of a sudden Zombie Uprising meeting, but it's the first one he's been to since you've known him.

❏ **3.** He's suddenly using the G'Oreal for Men cologne you'd given him—two years ago.

❏ **4.** He bought you an engraved heart necklace that says Best Friends Forever. Friends?

❏ **5.** He says sex is out because his penis is in danger of falling off, but you'd swear it felt pretty firm when you brushed by him earlier.

If he's an Angel:*

❏ **1.** There are bald patches in his wings, and they look suspiciously like well-manicured nail marks.

❏ **2.** His bedtime romps with you are suddenly un-Angelic and wickedly imaginative, prompting you to wonder where he's getting his ideas.

❏ **3.** He has to stay late for meetings with "The Big Guy" more and more often, not to mention all the extra flight time he's being asked to log—solo.

❏ **4.** His robe is dirty, but only at his knees.

❏ **5.** You find smudges of Perle Dust on him in spots he couldn't possibly reach.

If he's a Demon:

❏ **1.** He says, "I've been having sex with someone else. Want to join us?"

❏ **2.** He insists that those claw marks on his neck, chest, and back are from a ritual—but can't seem to remember what the ritual was for.

❏ **3.** He's got what looks suspiciously like rug burns on his back. And he's a Fire Demon.

❏ **4.** He claims he's too tired to act naughty.

❏ **5.** The local Demon hangout that you think of as your special place together no longer interests him and any time you walk past it, he ducks his head, as if afraid someone inside will see him. ❖

I know, everything you've heard about Angels tells you he'd never cheat—that's one of the things you love about him. But, as you've probably heard, sometimes even Angels fall . . . so check for these telltale signs.

Demonically
brilliant color to wake the dead

Rigor Mortis

Abra Cadaver

O (So) Negative

Gangrene

Halo

Black Plague

Bring out the Demon in your Angel or the Angel in your Demon with these smashing new nail shades, only from

DEVLON

Undead— and Gone!

Everything You Need to Know About When, Why, and How to Put a Stake in That Undead-End Relationship

It was all going so well. There were those "surprise" dates where he flew you off to Istanbul for dinner, followed by a stop in Rome for Blood Orange gelato; the romantic gifts of Nightshade Cologne and GoDieVa chocolates. (Remember when he told you that candy made your blood suck-ably sweet?) But lately . . . the bloom is off the rose. He has been forgetting important occasions like your birthday and Halloween. You've been arguing about little things like who drank the last can of Bludweiser or what he should wear when you visit your parents. ("Come on, honey—you have to wear *something!* And no biting the dog this time!") Those flirtatious little text messages he used to send you have degenerated into "Daylight Savings Time. Running late." Forever can be a long haul if you're stuck in an undead-end relationship. Is it time to cut your losses and move on? That's the eternal question—but we can help you answer it. The first step is spotting the signs that your romance is going down the wrong path.

Don't Let *This* ⟶ Turn Into *That*

Okay	Never Okay
A little bit forgetful ⟶	Doesn't return for days after a full moon
Slightly irritable ⟶	Says he's so hungry he could eat a human
Sometimes preoccupied with work ⟶	Brings home carcasses and stacks them in the garage so he can tinker after dinner
Inquisitive about your life ⟶	Stalks you relentlessly
Has to be reminded to help around the house ⟶	Leaves blood-soaked laundry or shredded clothing everywhere and snarls when you ask him to pick them up
Treasures his alone time ⟶	Comes home reeking of Wolfbane for Her, with suspicious scratches on his back and haunches

A Monster, or Just Being Himself?

The Immortox Quiz

Knowing when to break up isn't a big issue for immortals. They've got all the time in the world, after all. But you have to make plans—and if they don't include "HERS" and "ITS" towels hanging in your bathroom, you might as well face facts.

We've put together a simple quiz to help you determine if it's time to immortox your life and move on. Answer each question honestly, by circling the appropriate letter, then consult the scoring instructions at the end.

1. Your Werewolf sees you struggling with heavy packages but doesn't lift a paw to help. You think:

A. He views me as a strong, independent woman (which I am) and probably thinks I'd be insulted by his offer. It's sweet how much he respects me.

B. He's had such a hard night at the hunt. I don't blame him for letting me do the heavy lifting. In fact, when I'm done with this, I'll go get him a beer. One day he'll notice that I've had a hard day, too, and get me drinks while I sit on the couch.

C. Time to drop him.

D. Hmm, maybe he'll come if I just flash him a flirty smile and say, "Hey, you with all the muscles and hair. Want to help me with this stuff?"

The Facts

People in relationships help one another. Sure he wants to veg out like a Zombie at the end of the day, but the sight of you struggling should bring him bounding over to lend his massive strength. And if he seems a little slow on the uptake (a drawback of a few of the species), asking for his help is not out of line.

2. Your Vamp is a workaholic, spending all his time trying to enhance his already epic portfolio; or your Angel hangs out all day in the ozone with his celestial buddies, plotting new ways to impress You-Know-Who, excluding you completely. You think:

A. It's not easy to bring home the type O or get promoted to Archangel. And I wouldn't want his friends to tease him about being human-whipped.

B. If I show him how understanding I can be, he'll come around and start factoring me into his plans—starting with that Romanian getaway weekend he's been promising.

C. Time to *drop him*.

D. Pencil yourself in on his schedule for a little one-on-one at a hotel near where he works. Your Vamp's got to sleep, right? Then have room service deliver something tasty so you can spend time both in and out of bed.

The Facts

We're going to take the logical approach on this one. Any immortal who wants to be in a relationship with you will move heaven (if he's an Angel) or earth (if he's a Vamp gone to ground) to spend time with you. Sure, things come up, and you each have your own friends (at least you should). But there's a difference between being busy and being thoughtless. If his answer to you penciling your name on his day-planner is to pick up an eraser, you might want to consider Option C.

3. The immortal in your life has begun referring to you as "silly human," and not in that cute, teasing way. When you mention you'd like to go to grad school or learn to play the guitar, he laughs out loud. You think:

A. He's lived a long time and knows how hard it will be for me to reach my goals. He just wants to give me a realistic picture of what I'll be facing.

B. Who am I to think I can compete with him creatively or intellectually? He's lived forever, after all, and will always be better at everything.

C. Drop. Him.

D. Maybe I'll just remind my Zombie how much he hates it when I call him "meat bag." Then I'll flash him my most seductive smile and say that if he's ever going to enjoy a naked guitar serenade, he'll have to be a little more encouraging. That should work!

The Facts

There's a reason you're in a relationship with this super-dude, and it's just not the sex. It's nice to have someone in your corner, appreciating and supporting you (and not just feeding off of your bodily fluids). "Support" doesn't mean an enthusiastic green light on every idea, but you do need to ask yourself a few questions: Does your Were constantly chew through your goals and ambitions? Do you find yourself mentally creating a catalog of pros for your new venture in order to combat your Demon or Dragon's fiery counter-arguments? Do you come away from every conversation with your Vamp feeling stupid or bad about yourself?

If you can answer yes to even one of these questions, you might want to consider Option C. While it's nice to have your undead's input, no one has the right to make you feel bad about yourself.

4. Your guy may be immortal, but he's dead between the sheets. Not only have you not been having sex, but he finds all kinds of excuses to avoid your touch altogether. You think:

A. He may be a Were but he's not a circus animal ready to perform at my demand. When he's ready, it will happen. Or, my Vamp may be living in modern times, but he was born hundreds of years ago, when men were more inhibited and courtly. I'll just be patient a few hundred years longer . . .

B. He's right not to find me attractive. All of these late-night howls have left me bloated and tired-looking. Why would any creature want to touch me, let alone a handsome devil like him?

C. DROP HIM.

D. Tomorrow morning I am going to send him a naughty text, listing all of the infernal things I am dying to do to him—

and that I'm not wearing any panties today, just so I'll feel extra-specially sexy tonight! And if that doesn't do the trick, I will sweetly suggest that we should talk about our feelings and try to get closer again. Soon, I know he'll be his old, blood-thirsty self.

The Facts

If you think human guys are touchy, immortals have even more quirks when it comes to desire. But . . . men will be men, in this world and beyond. They love sex. So if your guy is losing interest at home, is it possible he's feeding elsewhere? (See the article on page 50 if you need help figuring this one out.) But if you really believe it is just a matter of turning up the heat, by all means, try everything you can think of to bring him back to life. In the end, if the eternal flame has gone out of your private life, it's probably not you—it's him. Time to find a creature who lights your fire, and vice versa.

. . . .

5. Your Angel is always nitpicking, criticizing "little things" about you, and pointing out ways you should change or be better. You think:

A. What's the big deal? He's using his centuries of knowledge to help me grow as a person. When he corrects my grammar so that I sound more Elizabethan, or reminds me that a well-brought-up girl always carries a fan, I should be grateful. He knows more about style than any of my friends or the current fashion magazines.

B. He is just pointing out what I know already . . . I am unworthy of dating an Angel, just like my mother said I was.

C. Time to drop him.

D. Hmm . . . the next time he complains about my cloud-keeping, I'm going to wink and say, let's blow out the candles and see how the place looks in the dark. I bet I can think of ways to distract you from the stardust on the altar . . .

The Facts

Holy is one thing, but nobody likes an Angel who is holier-than-thou. Constructive criticism in small doses is a plus when dating your moral ideal, but picking on you for every little thing is a sign that he doesn't respect your fabulous mortality. You might want to try reminding him of all the earthly tricks you've taught him . . . but if he continues to treat you like a human suggestion box, it might be time to fly.

KEY

If you've answered every question above honestly, it's time to tally up your score.

For every **A** answer, give yourself 1 point

For every **B** answer, give yourself 3 points

For every **C** answer give yourself 5 points

For every **D** answer, give yourself 10 points

5–11 points: You can rationalize anything and make excuses for the worst behavior. Be careful or you'll end up in the relationship graveyard.

12–20 points: Who told you that suffering was noble? One day he might see your goodness—but do you really have an eternity to find out?

21–35 points: Right on, girlfriend. You aren't going to take crud from anybody.

36 points and above: Self-esteem is a beautiful thing, especially when dating super-humans. You're unlikely to get bogged down with the wrong creature. ❖

This sassy, sexy Vampire knows… when real blood isn't an option, there's only one answer: Bludd. The delicious, nutritious, all-natural blood substitute will keep his cravings at bay when you're not in the mood (and keep him off you during that tricky time of the month). No LG's refrigerator is fully stocked without a few pints of Bludd for the Vamp in her life!

got bludd?

He's Gone— Now What?

Twelve Steps to Getting Over Him

1. Don't Let Him Continue to Feed

Ever hear one of your LG pals say how great she feels that she's still friends with an ex? She's lying. Hanging on is a sure sign that we are desperately hoping for a reconciliation.

So . . . when he's had one too many and rings your bell late at night, asking for "a little bite for old time's sake," slam that door. You'll thank yourself in the morning.

2. Make Yourself Look Fabulous

Whether you were the breaker or the breakee, looking fabulous is part of moving on. Get that pedicure, and paint your nails black because Angel's not around anymore to complain. Change your hairstyle (buns are definitely last-century) or splurge on that cute t-shirt that says MORTAL BUT CURIOUS. Get a total body wax (because, really, do you want to be reminded of fur?). This is the time to pamper yourself. You deserve it!

3. Stay Away from Old Haunts

When you break a heel, it's time to replace those old shoes with something strappier and cuter. It's the same with guys . . . don't shop in the same store twice! If you frequent the places you used to go with him, you'll end up making the same mistake all over again. Find a new place to hang out, and here's a tip: while getting over the breakup with your Were, avoid the moonlight. That's what got you into trouble in the first place.

4. Do That Thing He Hated

Fill in the blank: I haven't done _____ since we started dating. Now go do it! Now that your Demon is out of the picture, go and enjoy the hell out of the ballet. Mr. Vampire is in his coffin— time to hit the beach and work on your golden glow. Zombie's idea of "fine dining" was fish tacos at your place? Treat yourself to a blowout culinary experience (and ask them to cook the meat!). There's no better way to get over him than to reconnect with the pastimes (and people) you really like.

5. Deep Six His Stuff

Do you really need to be constantly reminded of your ex-Vamp when you walk through your apartment? Your office? It may seem like an innocent bottle of blood supplement he left at your place, but pretty soon you're twisting off the lid, closing your eyes and taking a swig (yuck!). You'll never get over your undead guy until you stow his photos, toss his extra change of cloak, and give away his favorite Goth recordings. He'll always be in your heart, but the sooner you get his junk out of your sight, the sooner he'll be out of your mind. And—if you are really heartsick and in need of an "immortox"—invite some friends over and make a big, old-fashioned cleansing pyre fueled by every item he ever gave you. Don't forget to roast a few marshmallows and sing some old camp songs! (If your ex is a Dragon, this ritual is NOT recommended, as it might just have the opposite effect and make you yearn for his fire.)

6. Don't Play With Fire

It's been a while. A little too long, and an LG has her needs. You begin thinking, "What's wrong with a quick fling with my ex, just for laughs (and screams)? It won't mean anything." Don't let the itch make you forget why you dropped your Demon and sent his no-strings booty-calling ass back to hell. Remember that old cliché about absence making the heart grow fonder? Well, it's true but dangerous. You're better off sticking with "out of sight, out of mind." Unless you want to risk having to start the healing process all over again, find a new guy to light your fire—maybe even a new species of guy.

7. LG Night Out!

Nothing jolts an LG out of her doldrums like a night out with the girls. Throw out that shredded, Werewolf-scented t-shirt that you've been sleeping in for the last three days, put on your killer heels, and call your pity posse. After ten minutes of commiserating and telling you that you're too good for him, they will drag your ass out for a great meal, a few drinks (not too many—see number 9), and some dancing at Hellfyre, where you can strut your stuff for the benefit of a whole new crop of otherworldly hotties. Seeing what's out there will bring you to your senses—and you might even meet the next Mr. Right.

8. Make a List, Check It Twice

As much as you try to dwell on his faults and the reasons for the breakup, your mind keeps going back to your Angel before he fell from grace. You start to think about the good times, the happy times . . . before his sanctimonious comments and nitpicking criticisms (and insistence on wearing white after Labor Day) started driving you crazy. Careful, ladies . . . your mind is playing tricks on you. Before you lose control and start drunk-dialing heaven, take out a piece of paper and make a list of all of his faults and shortcomings, along with every example of his disappointing, hurtful, or infuriating behavior. Get mad! Anger is a great help when it comes to healing—a lot better than sitting home and crying over reruns of *Touching an Angel.*

9. Don't Fall Too Far Off the Wagon

Drinking is a natural response to heartbreak—and it does feel good at first. One or two Dragontinis or Zombitas might elevate your mood and make you feel desirable to all of the other beasts in the forest . . . but after three or four, you could end up doing something you'll regret (and have to hide with RecoverGirl concealer). Do you really want a Property of <Your Ex's Name> tattoo on your arm—or butt? Watch your alcohol intake, and you'll never wake up with a strange phone number written on your wall in blood.

10. Run Like the Were

There's nothing like vigorous exercise to get him off your mind—and it'll get you back in shape for the hunt, too. Sure, give yourself a day or two to eat nothing but chocolate for breakfast, lunch, and dinner, but then grab those cute new running shorts and race like that Werewolf you no longer need!

11. Fly High

You might not be able to fly like your immortal ex, but that doesn't mean you can't reach new heights with a little "YOU" time for self-improvement. Take that Italian cooking class you always thought about (and throw away that *Braising Brains for Beginners* cookbook). Backpack across Europe (carefully avoiding Transylvania, of course). Not only will you reconnect with yourself and become happier, you'll develop great new skills and stories to try out on that future immortal who actually deserves you!

12. Find Someone New

Your bite marks have healed. You no longer look skyward for glimpses of your ex. You've moped. You've gotten over him. Pizza and cheesecake: done. Great pedicure and a night out with your best buds: check. Exercised off that five-pound bloat: double done. You're officially ready. In the end, the best revenge is a new-and-improved dream date—the one you are bound to find now that you've treated yourself the way you want him to treat you! ❖

Ten Ways to Keep Your Mortal Guy Pal
in the Friend Zone
(and His Mind Away from the End Zone!)

Your best friend is male and human, and you love him to pieces. But lately, it seems that he wants to share more than popcorn on movie night. WTF? Doesn't he understand that your taste is more . . . exotic? You'd rather donate a pint to your hot Vampire crush or go for a midnight romp in the underbrush with your Were than play tonsil hockey with Johnny Daytime.

How can you keep your normal-guy BFF happy (and accompanying you to movies and baseball games), yet discourage his romantic overtures? We've got some surefire ideas:

1. Make him buy you tampons—and don't be afraid to talk about your cramps.

2. Let yourself go. (No need to look alluring when you aren't luring anything.) Hair in a scrunchie, legs unshaved—anything goes.

3. Talk about other men—especially the drop-dead gorgeous immortals that fly or bound into view. Point out who's hot and ask if he thinks so, too.

4. Have a ready supply of chick flicks and foreign films every time he comes over for movie night or—even better—the complete *Twilight* saga. (WMD, use with caution: *Sex and the City 2*.)

5. Pat him on the head when you praise him. Werewolves love this, but it tends to remind a mortal guy of his mother.

6. Beg him to take care of you the next time you're sick—especially if you've got a stomach flu. (A word of caution: If he pulls this off, you might decide he's lover material after all.)

7. Throw a party and invite only your girlfriends—plus him. Then, try to set him up.

8. Hang pictures of your mother around the house and remind him you'll look just like her in a few decades.

9. Give him the Side Hug. This is the subtlest and kindest way to say, "You're not touching my breasts—ever."

10. Tell him all the reasons your last relationships failed. (Hint: "It was all that jerk's fault, blah, blah," self-pity galore.)

If he still wants you after all of that, you might have to banish him altogether and opt for an undead best bud. On that note, just how do you turn the immortal who craves you into a friend-for-eternity, and no more? We've got some tips for keeping your favorite beast in his place, too!

Wondering what to make for the Zombie of your dreams? Tired of bringing home Doritos and old laboratory animals? Whip up some Rot Pockets—now in his favorite flavors. The aroma alone will have him lurching off the couch and into the kitchen for a nibble!

Zombielicious!

Vampires

While humans have favorite foods, Vamps have favorite blood types. And now that synthetic blood is being marketed to the fangers, you can head to your local grocery, pick up a hated vial of B neg, blend in a little garlic, and vavoom! You've got a recipe sure to keep his teeth in someone else's neck. For extra fang-blocking, don't be afraid to mix your favorite bath oil or perfume with holy water.

Werewolves

Apply a tiny dollop of catnip behind each ear, or, if you really want to offend his delicate sniffer, include it in your fabric softener. Secret weapon: Weres are notoriously allergic to silver, so bring on the bling. Silver earrings, headbands, bangles, and beads need to be your new favorite accessories.

Zombies

First thing, cut off his supply of sugary cereal and swap in healthy vegetarian snacks such as carrot sticks and tofu dip. If that doesn't work, send your couch out to be cleaned and replace it temporarily with an exer-cycle. Knowing Zombies, he'll wander off, have a few beers, and forget about you—but soon enough, you can call him and hang out again, no hard feelings (or memory of what happened).

Dragons

Fire-breathers can be single-minded and prideful to a fault, so take the direct and forceful approach. Tell him you care for him but only as a friend. This is sure to make his wings droop for a while. His classic Dragon pride will probably keep him from trying to seduce you after that, though he might try to make you jealous by dating your best friend. If you think you need more ammunition to drive home your point, watch a few Dragon movies with him and cheer for the slayer.

Angels

Say hello to your fake (but real-looking) tattoo, right where he's sure to notice it. We recommend some-thing naughty, such as the insignia for a local biker club or the ever-popular *I Love Mustache Rides*. Alternatively, don a saffron robe and start chanting—though this might make him turn his other cheek permanently.

Demons

These guys are perhaps the easiest to dissuade. Bible? Check. Crosses on the wall? Check, check. And if those don't turn him off, just drop the "C" word. *Commitment.* He'll be looking for his carnal kicks elsewhere before you can say "great balls o' fire." ❖

"Is It Hot in This Dungeon— or Is It YOU?"

Immortal Icebreakers Sure to Turn His Undead Head

If you think killer pickup lines are only for guys, think again. We girls have to know how to pounce, too! Say you are at your favorite after-hours hangout and *he* flies in: the Vamp of your dreams. You check him out, from the twinkle in his dark-red eyes (a signal of his hunger) to the points of his shiny black boots. His smile offers a hint of fang and his body language tells you that he could be yours for the asking. Without thinking, you readjust your collar to show a little more clavicle. What are you going to say?

Here are a few ideas for supernatural conversation-starters . . . just to spark your imagination. With some thought, you'll come up with your own assortment of immortal icebreakers sure to captivate his attention and charm the leather pants or choir robes right off him (if that's what you're after)—or at least guarantee that your next Angeltini is covered.

Vampires

- Greetings and salivations!

- Hi, I'm new in town—can you give me directions to your castle?

- That cape would look great in a crumpled heap next to my bed.

- Do you believe in love at first bite—or should I let you nibble on me over and over again?

- If it's true that we are what we eat, then you could be me by morning!

Zombies

- They say this bar is a meat market . . . well, I'd love to be your prime rib.

- Apart from being sexy, what exactly do Zombies do for a living?

- I've just moved you to the top of my to-do list.

- I've heard sex with a Zombie is a killer, and I'm ready to die happy.

Werewolves

- Are Werewolves from Tennessee? Because you're the only ten I see!

- The moon isn't full tonight, but I bet I can make you howl.

- You might be a wolf, but *I'm* invisible. What? You can see me? Well, how about you see me tomorrow night, too?

- You know what would look great on me? Your paws.

Angels

- Don't mind me—I'm an astronomer checking out heavenly bodies.

- I hope Angels know CPR—because you take my breath away.

- I'll have coffee. Hold the sugar, and dip your little finger in it for me.

- Am I dead, Angel-face? Because those wings are heavenly.

Dragons

- Hope that torch you're carrying is for me.

- Dragons must be great thieves—you stole my heart from across the room!

- Whoever said, "never play with fire," hasn't seen that flame-thrower of yours.

- If you were a new item at Burger King, you'd be a McHottie—and I'd have you my way!

Demons

- I think I have a little Demon in me—at least I hope to by the end of the night!

- What has lots of teeth, isn't a Vampire, but needs to be taken down a notch? Your zipper!

- Excuse me, handsome, I think I dropped something. My jaw!

- Are you going to kiss me—or do I have to lie to my diary? ❖

Manscaping Your Manly Immortal

Hair- and Skincare Help He'll Positively Die For, from the Otherworldly Prince of Products
by Sebastian Heath

BEFORE

AFTER

Many immortal guys get top marks for their grooming prowess, but there's also a pack of them out there who seem to have lost interest in making an effort about a hundred years ago. Broaching the subject with your man can be a tricky thing, but if the only reason you want to sink your fingers into his hair is because his 'do is groan-worthy, it's time to work out your battle plan.

Subtle doesn't cut it. If your man is a little slow on the uptake (and he probably is), just flat out tell him how great he'd look with sharply polished horns/shaped eyebrows/less ear hair/whiter fangs. No immortal will turn down the chance to hear how great he is from your lips, over and over again.

Minimize his opportunities to retreat. As much as your guy likes to look tough and strong in front of you, no member of the otherworld wants a pair of tweezers heading straight for something that is firmly attached. Here's where you . . .

Offer to do it for him. With the right props, an immortal will read this as something you can do *to* him. So strap on a blood red corset, straddle his hips, and he'll wonder . . . what unibrow?

Surprise Attack. Once again, props are your best friends. Pull on a pair of black stockings, clear heels—bra and panties are optional—and gift him with a basket of products. He'll remember your hotness every time he uses the hair gel and cologne.

Sneak Attack. This is the sly version of the surprise attack. You just simply place (or replace) in plain sight any of the great products you want him to use. Place a sexy picture of yourself or a suggestive note you've written underneath. Example: *Use this, then come find me* . . . . He'll be more than happy to obey.

Which brings me to products. Here are some of my favorites!

For the Dragon in your life, **Sc'Olay for Men**. This foaming body wash is perfect for that big guy's scales and with an SPF of over 90, he can flame all night long!

Tired of not being able to stroke your Demon's horns? I guarantee he is! Now there's **Horneline**. This is one form of protection that actually increases the sensation!

Your Angel may have fallen from heaven, but that doesn't mean his hair can't still be wind resistant. This product puts the found in your **Lost Angel Locks**.

He may come from the Middle Ages, but your Vamp doesn't have to smell like it. Now there's **Old Vice**: to turn him back into the man he used to smell like!

Just because he's enjoying the afterlife, doesn't mean he can't taste minty fresh, too. When it comes to Zombies, nothing beats **Afterline**! And with its cavity fighting agents, he can eat all the sweets he craves.

And for your Werewolf, I recommend **PAC styling gel**, sure to give him that bedhead look you both crave!

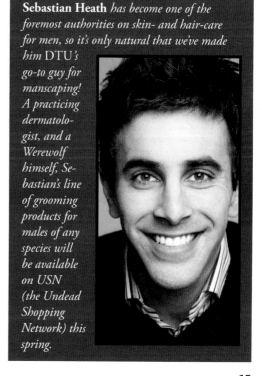

Sebastian Heath *has become one of the foremost authorities on skin- and hair-care for men, so it's only natural that we've made him DTU's go-to guy for manscaping! A practicing dermatologist, and a Werewolf himself, Sebastian's line of grooming products for males of any species will be available on USN (the Undead Shopping Network) this spring.*

JIMMY CHEW

Howlin' Hot Fashion Makeovers That Take Him from Frightening to Fashionable

Taming Your Savage Beast's Wardrobe While Letting His Freak Flag Fly!

While most immortals are class acts all the way—and that includes their smokin' wardrobes—some of them do need our help. (They are *men*, after all.) Broaching the subject of a fashion makeover with your immortal can be a tricky thing, but if the only reason you want to rip off his clothes is that his outfit is groan-worthy, it's time to have the talk. Just because your Vamp can't see himself in a mirror doesn't mean others aren't watching. And what about your Were? Being a wolf and looking like he's been dragged in by one are two very different things. What about the burn holes in your Dragon-Shifter's favorite jeans? There's the distressed look, and then there's the just plain painful look.

Don't be afraid to sit him down and woo him with phrases like, "Your buff Dragon body would look even more amazing in a tailored suit," or, "I love the way your eyes glow when you're about to go native. I saw a sexy cashmere sweater the other day that would make your eyes pop that way all the time."

Or, pick up a men's fashion mag, then, while reading it in front of him, casually mention, "You're such a hottie. I bet you could rock some of these hot designer duds better than these scrawny mortal models."

You can build up to the idea of a makeover slowly, too. When you're out and about together and see a nicely dressed guy, make a comment like, "That's a great jacket that guy has on, but a hot Demon like you would totally kill it!" If he's a Vampire, try comparing his style to that of a well-dressed Werewolf. Something like, "I love the pants that Werewolf has on. Too bad they don't make them for Vampires." Chances are he'll leap at the opportunity to show you how progressive Vampire style can be.

Unfortunately, sometimes subtle doesn't cut it. If your guy is on the dense side, take him with you when you go shopping and let one of the sales staff offer a few off-the-cuff-but-preplanned statements about how great he'd look in a new suit or a more fashionable pair of jeans. Amazing what the suggestions of a professional can accomplish.

Ultimately, seeing your excitement and wanting to please you should be enough to get him to the nearest men's boutique. Just remember not to push things too far until he's ready. Respect his individuality, and stay true to his core identity. Putting a Werewolf biker in a three-piece pinstriped getup isn't going to work (especially when he shifts), but a comfortable, relaxed pair of linen or silk drawstring pants might really appeal to him when you point out how great they feel and how easy they are to shed.

Some tips to try and things to remember:

• Rome (as he will tell you) wasn't built in a day. Don't get him one new outfit and expect to wake up next to George Clooney. Unless you're already sleeping with George Clooney, and in that case, why do you care what he's wearing? And is it true he's a Vampire? He does seem ageless . . .

• Help him shop, making sure to take into consideration his need for tail or wing accessibility, SPF factors, or fire resistance. Doing that will really cut down on his reasons for not trying something new. In theory, if you fill his closet with appropriate choices, he'll do much better at dressing himself on a daily basis.

• It can be really tough for a guy to make appropriate choices when the best stores are closing just as he's waking up. Introduce your Vampire to the world of online retail!

• Reward him when he looks good. (And by that we mean well dressed—immortals always look good in the buff.) You do know what we mean by reward, right? We're talking about a night that is so hot and steamy, he'll be putty in your hands when it comes time for that next shopping trip.

• Don't be afraid to enlist the help of a personal shopper. Many high-end department stores are now offering a one-on-one service that specifically caters to the needs of immortals: late-night hours and a staff that includes immortals themselves, assuring an intimate knowledge of your man's needs—needs he might be too embarrassed to discuss with you.

• For the Vampire who can't ditch his leather and velvet or the Demon who won't leave home without his ceremonial robe, go slowly but be firm. Letting him know that velvet is better suited for coffin lining than pants and that robes are what the Angels prefer should help. And don't forget, there's room in every man's wardrobe for a smart leather jacket. ❖

One more thing. Always err on the side of preparedness:

For Vamps, bloodstains can be a bitch. Make sure you carry some Fiendout Wipes or a BloodTide Stain Stick in your purse.

Weres sometimes shift into their animal form without warning. They need clothing that falls from their furry bodies easily. A dog in underwear? Not pretty.

With Dragons, fire-resistant material goes a long way toward keeping your man dressed all night—but don't forget to carry cologne. Smoke will never be the scent of the day.

One word when it comes to Zombies: Spandex. There is now a line of clothing designed specifically with Zombies in mind, with cinches around the shoulders, elbows, and knees and a high percentage of that very necessary, clinging fabric, allowing him to feel confident about his body all night long.

Angels are notorious neat freaks and do not like to leave their fallen feathers behind. Make sure his clothing has pockets lots and lots of pockets. Otherwise, you'll never get him out of his heavenly robe.

As much as your fiendish Demon loves to have sex—in public, in private, anywhere, everywhere—you'll delight his black heart and soul if you surprise him with the new Pantlettes. These tiny towels easily attach to the inside of his pants, around the zipper area. When he unleashes his beast, the material unfolds to ensure his pants stay clean and dry.

One last note: With all these changes you are urging on him, your guy might feel like the time is right to talk to you about some of your own less than desirable styles. Many immortals prefer a more subtle look than their LGs are accustomed to sporting. Be prepared to ditch a few things for him, like that Team Edward shirt (you're really still wearing that?) or the croc-embossed handbag that's a little too close for comfort for your Dragon-Shifter. Above all, be gracious about making the changes, just as you want him to be. Who knows, you might learn something about your man's taste and what turns him on!

Vamp Stamps and Real-Life Dragon Tattoos

We Found a Host of Heavenly Bodies Displaying Their Passion in the Most Unlikely Places!

What better way to celebrate your unearthly desires than to wear them on your sleeve…literally?

Our intrepid street photographers snapped a bevy of beauties letting their dark side come out to play—in the form of some very special body art. Shoulders adorned with Angel wings, flames of dragon fire licking lovely midsections, playful bite and nibble marks on innocent necks… there is no end to the ingenuity of an LG with an otherworldly itch.

Thinking about getting inked but not sure where to start? We asked our gal-on-the-street models to say a little something about their very special body art. Check it out!

"I'd been dating my Angel for over a year when I decided to surprise him with my 'angel wings.' He was so surprised, he wept! It sounds silly, but I really believe that my wings have brought us closer together—and definitely closer to heaven."

"This ancient symbol for love has really gotten me noticed at clubs—especially by those smokin' Demons down at The Lair. To me, it says, 'Sure, I'm Demon bait—but I know how to take care of myself so keep that burner on simmer until I give the word!'"

"That's right—Draco, the sign of the Dragon. If you know anything about immorstrology, then you know that dating a Draco can make a girl's head spin—but take it from me, it's worth it! As fiery, moody, and unpredictable as they can be, they are the only guys who make my blood run hot, and my tattoo lets the world (and *them*) know it. One glimpse of my bicep and those fire-breathers are lining up to toast my marshmallows!"

"Made you look twice, right? These 'bite marks' are a tribute to the Vamp I dated and tragically lost in a freak staking accident. I missed him so much, a friend suggested getting a tattoo as a way to remember and honor him. She was right! Every time I catch a glimpse of my reflection, I think about his lips pressed against my skin and shiver. I'll never forget him, and now any man in my life knows I've been with a true gentleman and so he should treat me like a lady. Well, except while we're in bed."

"It sounds crazy, but I feel more alive since I got these flames! They were actually a birthday present from the very special Zombie in my life. He wanted me to know I'm the light of his life and that his passion burns bright. (I didn't tell him it's the sign of the Dragons. Shhhh!) I was a little bit nervous to take the plunge and I still haven't shown my parents, but since I got them, our love life . . . well . . . let's just say he likes to lick the ink and leave it at that."

Eternally Yours
Unique Gifts Sure to ⟡ Melt His Immortal Heart

It's hard enough to buy for the average guy, but buying for an immortal who's had years to shop for himself (and who is riddled with the quirks inherent in his species) sometimes seems downright impossible. Never fear—we've chosen a range of gifts designed not only to let him know you care, but to show him that you're paying attention to his special needs! What's more, we know you have to watch your wallet.

Some occasions call for a splurge while others necessitate just a thoughtful little token. So, for each creature out there, we've selected gifts in the "luxury," "generous," and "pennywise" category. If none of our ideas do the trick for you, perhaps they will spark your imagination to come up with a gift that will make his eyes light up in the dark!

Vampires

Luxury: The Harley Davidson Fat Boy with the Impaler package can't be beat for hot rides for undead guys. This bike features a specially equipped set of saddlebags: one carries a pop-up UV shelter that can be erected in less than thirty seconds, while the other is wired to act as a cooler, making blood transportation without spoilage a snap.

Generous: Luxotica Skin Renewal Crème. This blood-red cream isn't pretty, but Luxotica Skin Renewal is specially formulated for Vampires. Made from a proprietary blend of human and animal plasma plus some other secret ingredients, it literally brings new life to undead skin. It may seem pricey at about $120 a pint, but a little goes a long way.

Pennywise: Flowers. Yes, we said flowers. While he can buy these for himself, he probably won't, and when we took a recent Vampire survey, an overwhelming number said they missed the smell of a sunny day. Flowers are a great way to let him know you understand!

Werewolves

Luxury: Herz-filtering Earbuds. These top-of-the-line earplugs use modern technology and a touch of magic to filter out the high 20,000Hz to 48,000Hz sounds that are inaudible to human ears but painfully piercing to canine ones. (Think dog whistles.) The best part about these earbuds is that besides being nearly invisible when worn, they don't filter out the normal range of human hearing, so all other sounds are crystal clear. If he says he didn't hear you, tell him you know better.

Generous: Nothing gives a great shine to a Were's coat like a genuine boar-bristle brush. And if you've never helped your guy with a little hands-on grooming before, you'll soon see why this gift is fun for both of you.

Pennywise: Caffeinated Soap. After a long night spent howling at the moon, your guy might need a little extra get-up-and-go. The caffeine in this soap is absorbed through the skin, making his morning shower that much more invigorating!

Dragons

Luxury: The Howlex Draikon. This watch sports five-and-a-half carats of the kind of sparkle that's a guaranteed Dragon-magnet. We know how much Dragons like bling, so why not reward that great guy with a watch he can stare at to his fiery heart's content? Be sure to engrave the back with a special message just for him! ("Light my fire" has been done to death—you can come up with something better than that!)

Generous: Tears of the Gods. Yes, yes, we know. This ultra cooling medicated gel is marketed to Angels, since they sometimes do battle with Demons and end up with burnt patches on their wings. And yes, Dragons love some heat and fire. But, the acid-like chemicals in their saliva can burn even *their* scales—saliva that can drip onto their hands when they are about to flame. No one enjoys a scabbed-over wound. A tube of Tears of the Gods will say you understand his subtlest needs.

Pennywise: Auntie Liza's Scale Polish. If your guy is looking a little dull, a rub down with Auntie Liza's is just the trick! He'll be gleaming and grateful in no time. And you'll be the LG to thank.

Zombies

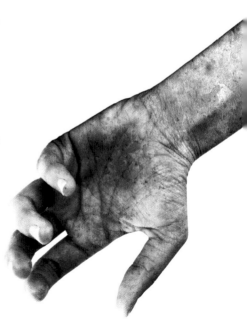

Luxury: Zombieland. No, not the movie, the exclusive retreat! A week for two at this spa resort isn't cheap, but it's so worth it. It takes a specialist to correctly massage a Zombie, and this place not only has them, they'll train you in their mysterious arts in a special hands-on couples class. Every activity and amenity is designed with the Zombie in mind. It's a great place to get to know each other better and bond while your every need—and his—are taken care of!

Generous: Xander's Xtra-Limb. Nothing ruins an evening out with your Zombie like an arm that suddenly detaches. Yes, it happens. Stash one of these Xtra-Limbs in your guy's glove box or your purse and he'll never have to wonder how he's going to fill out his shirtsleeve again! Made of a space-age polymer that goes from egg-sized capsule to life-size limb just by cracking the tiny pocket of activator inside each container, Xtra-Limbs really show the Zombie in your life how much you care about him and his appearance. And let's face it, appearance can be a major hurdle when you're dating a Zombie to begin with.

Pennywise: There's a whole new line of fun t-shirts out there just for Zombies. Our favorite is the one with the saying, "If you can read this, thank me for not eating your brains." Silly, sure, but that's the kind of humor Zombies appreciate. And it makes perfect lounging-around-the-house wear.

Angels

Luxury: Angelo Vetro, a glass manufacturer in Italy, will hand-craft a replica of your Angel (from wing to toe) in Murano glass based on photographs. They have a secret process in which they inlay a variety of precious gems and ribbons of fine metal. Sizes range from tabletop to life-size, but they're always stunning. A real museum piece.

Generous: Perle Dust. This is a fun gift for both you and your Angelic other. Perle Dust is made from an ancient secret formula, and gives an Angel's wings an amazing, extra-special glow. Use a little on yourself (think body glitter) and the dust's properties will make you irresistible to him! It isn't the easiest to find, but if you have a Chinese apothecary in your city, chances are good they'll be able to procure it for you. As an aside, this magical stuff also kills and controls feather mites—but just pretend you don't know that.

Pennywise: Name A Star. Sure, naming a star after him through the International Star Registry might sound a little corny, but just because he comes from heaven doesn't mean he owns a piece of it. He'll appreciate the thought behind this sweet gift, too.

Demons

Luxury: Diamond and Platinum horn caps. These gorgeous, blingy circlets are custom made to sit securely on the tips of his horns, whatever their girth. All you have to do is measure them with a piece of string while he's sleeping and send it in! Demons love a bit of sparkle, so if your budget allows, go crazy and get a pair of these made for him. Plus, these have the added benefit of protecting you from any poison those horns of his might leak, allowing you to finally toss out those flavored horn condoms!

Generous: Dremel's horn polishing attachment. This diamond-powder-embedded polishing wheel will bring the shine back to even the most battle-scarred horns. And since a Demon's horns are a well-known erogenous zone, you'll want to use it together. In fact, if you actually manage to get both horns polished on the same night, you're either doing something wrong or downing stamina potions! A nice secondary use for the polishing wheel is as a file for those quick-growing claws and talons when a trip to the manicurist won't fit into his schedule.

Pennywise: Hellsbane Bubble Bath. Nothing gets rid of that sulphury Demon smell like Hellsbane. And while the gift alone might not be the sexiest thing, sharing a hot bath sure is!

Time to Update His Look!
J. CRUD

Your Vamp's clothes were the height of fashion in the 19th century, but perhaps his style is getting a little bit…musty? Or maybe your Zom is a bit shaggy and shabby, even for a Zom. No problem! J. Crud has everything to turn your undead darling into a dandy—just in time for dinner at your parents'!

Hard to fit (or hard to please)? We can handle it!

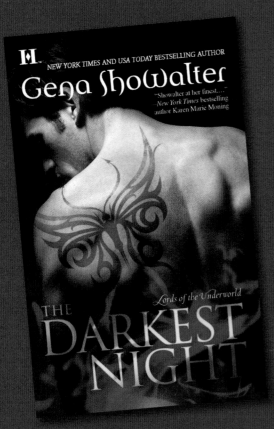

Fiction Classic!
Is Maddox the most dangerous
Lord of the Underworld ever—
or just the sexiest? The story
begins here . . .

The Darkest Night

Set in Budapest, with its old-world charm and modern-day mystique, *The Darkest Night* is the first novel in Gena Showalter's best selling Lords of the Underworld series—the one that started it all. Check out Chapter One of this classic, and help us decide if Maddox, keeper of the demon of Violence, is the most dangerous warrior living in the demon fortress—or just the sexiest.

CHAPTER ONE

EVERY NIGHT DEATH CAME, slowly, painfully, and every morning Maddox awoke in bed, knowing he'd have to die again later. That was his greatest curse and his eternal punishment.

He ran his tongue over his teeth, wishing it were a blade over his enemy's throat instead. Most of the day had already passed. He'd heard the time seep away, a poisonous tick-tock in his mind, every beat of the clock a mocking reminder of mortality and pain.

In little more than an hour, the first sting would pierce his stomach and nothing he did, nothing he said, would change that. Death *would* come for him.

"Damned gods," he muttered, increasing the speed of his bench presses.

"Bastards, every one of them," a familiar male voice said from behind him.

Maddox's motions didn't slow at Torin's unwelcome intrusion. Up. Down. Up. Down. For two hours he had worked out his frustration and anger on the punching bag, the treadmill and now the weights. Sweat ran from his bare chest and arms, riding the ropes of his muscles in clear rivulets. He should be as exhausted mentally as he was physically, but his emotions were only growing darker, more powerful.

> In a little more than an hour, the first sting would pierce his stomach and nothing he did, nothing he said, would change that. Death *would* come for him.

"You should not be here," he said.

Torin sighed. "Look. I didn't mean to interrupt, but something's happened."

"So take care of it."

"I can't."

"Whatever it is, try. I'm in no shape to help." These last few weeks very little was needed to send him into a killing haze where no one around him was safe. Even his friends. *Especially* his friends. He didn't want to, never meant to, but was sometimes helpless against urges to strike and to maim.

"Maddox—"

"I'm at the edge, Torin," he croaked. "I would do more harm than good."

Maddox knew his limitations, had known them for thousands of years. Ever since that doomed day the gods had chosen a woman to perform a task that should have been his.

Pandora had been strong, yes, the strongest female soldier of their time. But he had been stronger. More capable. Yet he had been deemed too weak to guard *dimOuniak,* a sacred box housing demons so vile, so destructive, they could not even be trusted in Hell.

As if Maddox would have allowed it to be destroyed. Frustration had bloomed inside him at the affront. Inside all of them, every warrior now living here. They had fought diligently for the king of the gods, killed expertly and protected thoroughly; they should have been chosen as guards. That they hadn't was an embarrassment not to be tolerated.

They'd only thought to teach the gods a lesson the night they'd stolen *dimOuniak* from Pandora and released that horde of demons upon the unsuspecting world. How foolish they had been. Their plan to prove their power had failed, for the box had gone missing in the fray, leaving the warriors unable to recapture a single evil spirit.

Destruction and havoc had soon reigned, plunging the world into darkness until the king of the gods finally intervened, cursing each warrior to house a demon inside *himself.*

A fitting punishment. The warriors had unleashed the evil to avenge their stinging pride; now they would contain it.

And so the Lords of the Underworld were born.

Maddox had been given Violence, the demon who was now as much a part of him as his lungs or his heart. Now, man could no longer live without demon and demon could no longer function without man. They were woven together, two halves of a whole.

From the very first, the creature inside him had beckoned him to do malicious things, hated things, and he'd been compelled to obey. Even when led to slay a woman—to slay Pandora. His fingers clenched the bar so tightly his knuckles nearly snapped out of place. Over the years he had learned to control some of the demon's more vile compulsions, but it was a constant struggle and he knew he could shatter at any moment.

What he would have given for a single day of calm. No overpowering desire to hurt others. No battles within himself. No worries. No death. Just . . . peace.

"It's not safe for you here," he told his friend, who still stood in the doorway. "You need to leave." He set the silver bar atop its perch and sat up. "Only Lucien and Reyes are allowed to be close to me during my demise." And only because they played a part in it, unwilling though they were. They were as helpless against their demons as Maddox was his.

"About an hour until that happens, so . . ." Torin threw a rag at him. "I'll take my chances."

Maddox reached behind his back, caught the white cloth and turned. He wiped his face. "Water."

An ice-cold bottle was soaring through the air before the second syllable left his mouth. He caught it deftly, moisture splashing his chest. He drained the icy contents and studied his friend.

As usual, Torin wore all black and gloves covered his hands. Pale hair fell in waves to his shoulders, framing a face mortal females considered a sensual feast. They didn't know the man was actually a devil in angel's skin. They should have, though. He practically glowed with irreverence, and there was an unholy gleam in his green eyes that proclaimed he would laugh in your face while cutting out your

heart. Or laugh in your face while you cut out *his* heart. To survive, he had to find humor where he could. They all did.

Like every resident of this Budapest fortress, Torin was damned. He might not die every night like Maddox, but he could never touch a living thing, skin to skin, without infecting it with sickness.

> As usual, Torin wore all black and gloves covered his hands. Pale hair fell in waves to his shoulders, framing a face mortal females considered a sensual feast.

Torin was possessed by the spirit of Disease.

He hadn't known a woman's touch in over four hundred years. He'd learned his lesson well when he'd given in to lust and caressed a would-be lover's face, bringing about a plague that decimated village after village. Human after human.

"Five minutes of your time," Torin said, his determination clear. "That's all I'm asking."

"Think we'll be punished for insulting the gods today?" Maddox replied, ignoring the request. If he didn't allow himself to be asked for a favor, he didn't have to feel guilty for turning it down.

His friend uttered another of those sighs. "Our every breath is supposed to be a punishment."

True. Maddox's lips curled into a slow, razored smile as he peered ceilingward. *Bastards. Punish me further, I dare you.* Maybe then, finally, he would fade to nothingness.

He doubted the gods would concern themselves, though. After bestowing the death-curse upon him, they had ignored him, pretending not to hear his pleas for forgiveness and absolution. Pretending not to hear his promises and desperate bargaining.

What more could they do to him, anyway?

Nothing could be worse than dying over and over again. Or being stripped of anything good and right . . . or hosting the spirit of Violence inside his mind and body.

Jackknifing to his feet, Maddox tossed the now-wet rag and empty water bottle into the nearest hamper. He strode to the far end of the room and braced his hands above his head, leaning into the semicircular alcove of stained-glass windows and staring into the night through the only clear partition.

He saw Paradise.

He saw hell.

He saw freedom, prison, everything and nothing.

He saw . . . home.

Situated atop a towering hill as the fortress was, he had a direct view of the city. Lights glowed brightly, pinks, blues and purples illuminating the murky velvet sky, glinting off the Danube River and framing the snowcapped trees that dominated the area. Wind blustered, snowflakes dancing and twirling through the air.

Here, he and the others had a modicum of privacy from the rest of the world. Here, they were allowed to come and go without having to face a barrage of questions. *Why don't you age? Why do screams echo through the forest every night? Why do you sometimes look like a monster?*

> Here, he and the others had a modicum of privacy from the rest of the world. Here, they were allowed to come and go without having to face a barrage of questions.

Here, the locals maintained their distance, awed, respectful. "Angels," he'd even heard whispered during a rare encounter with a mortal.

If they only knew.

Maddox's nails elongated slightly, digging into the stone. Budapest was a place of majestic beauty, old-world charm and modern pleasures, but he'd always felt removed from it. From the castle district that lined one street to the nightclubs that lined the next. From the fruits and vegetables hawked in one alley to the living flesh hawked in the other.

Maybe that sense of disconnection would vanish if he ever explored the city, but unlike the others who roamed at will, he was trapped inside the fortress and surrounding land as surely as Violence had been trapped inside Pandora's box thousands of years ago.

His nails lengthened farther, almost claws now. Thinking of the box always blackened his mood. *Punch a wall,* Violence beckoned. *Destroy something. Hurt, kill.* He would have liked to obliterate the gods. One by one. Decapitate them, perhaps. Rip out their blackened, decayed hearts, definitely.

The demon purred in approval.

Of course it's purring now, Maddox thought with disgust. Anything bloodthirsty, no matter the victims, met with the creature's support. Scowling, he leveled another heated glance at the heavens. He and the demon had been paired long ago, but he remembered the day clearly. The screams of the innocent in his ears, humans bleeding all around him, hurting, dying, the spirits having devoured their flesh in a rapturous frenzy.

Only when Violence had been shoved inside his body did he lose touch with reality. There had been no sounds, no sights. Just an all-consuming darkness. He hadn't regained his senses until Pandora's blood splattered his chest, her last breath echoing in his ears.

She had not been his first kill—or his last—but she had been the first and only woman to meet his sword. The horror of seeing that once-vibrant female form broken and knowing he was responsible for it . . . . To this day, he had not assuaged the guilt, the regret. The shame and the sorrow.

He'd sworn to do whatever was necessary to control

the spirit from then on, but it had been too late. Enraged all the more, Zeus had bestowed a second curse upon him: every night at midnight he would die exactly as Pandora had died—a blade through the stomach, six hellish times. The only difference was, her torment had ended within minutes.

His torment would last for eternity.

He popped his jaw, trying to relax against a new onslaught of aggression. It wasn't as if he were the only one to suffer, he reminded himself. The other warriors had their own demons—literally and figuratively. Torin, of course, was keeper of Disease. Lucien was keeper of Death. Reyes, of Pain. Aeron, of Wrath. Paris, of Promiscuity.

Why couldn't *he* have been given that last one? He would have been able to journey to town anytime he wished, take any woman he desired, savoring every sound, every touch.

As it was, he could never venture far. Nor could he trust himself around females for long periods of time. If the demon overtook him or if he could not return home before midnight and someone found his dead, bloody body and buried him—or worse, burned him . . . .

How he wished such a thing would end his miserable existence. He would have left long ago and allowed himself to be roasted in a pit. Or perhaps he would have jumped from the fortress's highest window and smashed his brains from his skull. But no. No matter what he did, he'd merely awaken once again, charred as well as sore. Broken as well as sliced.

"You've been staring at that window for a while," Torin said. "Aren't you even curious as to what's happened?"

Maddox blinked as he was dragged from his thoughts. "You're still here?"

His friend arched a black brow, the color a startling contrast to his silver-white hair. "I believe the answer to my question is no. Are you calm now, at least?"

Was he ever truly calm? "As calm as a creature like me can be."

"Stop whining. There's something I need to show you, and don't try to deny me this time. We can talk about my reason for disturbing you along the way." Without another word, Torin spun on his booted heel and strode from the room.

Maddox remained in place for several seconds, watching his friend disappear around the corner. *Stop whining,* Torin had said. Yes, that's exactly what he had been doing. Curiosity and wry amusement pushed past his lethal mood, and Maddox stepped from the gym into the hallway. A cold draft of air swirled around him, thick with moisture and the crisp scents of winter. He spied Torin a few feet away and stalked forward, quickly closing in.

"What's this about?"

"Finally. Interest," was the only response.

"If this is one of your tricks…" Like the time Torin had ordered hundreds of blow-up dolls and placed them throughout the fortress, all because Paris had foolishly complained about the lack of female companionship in town. The plastic "ladies" had stared out from every corner, their wide eyes and let-me-suck-you mouths taunting everyone who passed them.

> Like the time Torin had ordered hundreds of blow-up dolls and placed them throughout the fortress, all because Paris had foolishly complained about the lack of female companionship in town.

Things like that happened when Torin was bored.

"I wouldn't waste my time trying to trick you," Torin said without turning to face him. "You, my friend, have no sense of humor."

True.

As Maddox kept pace, stone walls stretched at his sides; sconces glowed, pulsing with light and fire, twining shadow with gold. The House of the Damned, as Torin had dubbed the place, had been built hundreds of years ago.

Though they had modernized it as best they could, the age showed in the crumbling rock and the scuffed floors.

> As Maddox kept pace, stone walls stretched at his sides; sconces glowed, pulsing with light and fire, twining shadow with gold.

"Where is everyone?" Maddox asked, only then realizing he hadn't spotted any of the others.

"You'd think Paris would be shopping for food since our cabinets are nearly bare and that's his only duty, but no. He's out searching for a new woman."

Lucky bastard. Possessed as he was by Promiscuity, Paris could not bed the same woman twice, and so he seduced a new one—or two or three—every day. The only downside? If he couldn't find a woman, he was reduced to doing things Maddox didn't even want to contemplate. Things that left the normally good-tempered man hunched over a toilet, heaving the contents of his stomach. Though Maddox's envy abated at such moments, it always returned when Paris spoke of one of his lovers. The soft brush of a thigh . . . the meeting of hot skin . . . the groans of ecstasy . . . .

"Aeron is . . . prepare yourself," Torin began, "because this is the main reason I hunted you down."

"Did something happen to him?" Maddox demanded as darkness shuttered over his thoughts and anger overtook him. *Destroy, obliterate,* Violence beseeched, clawing at the corners of his mind. "Is he hurt?"

Immortal Aeron might be, but he could still be harmed. Even killed—a feat they had all discovered in the worst possible way.

"Nothing like that," Torin assured him.

Slowly, he relaxed and gradually Violence receded. "What, then? Cleaning a mess and throwing a fit?" Every warrior here had specific responsibilities. It was their way of maintaining some semblance of order amid the chaos of their own souls. Aeron's task was maid service, something he complained about on a daily basis. Maddox took care of home repairs. Torin played with stocks and bonds, whatever those were, keeping them well-moneyed. Lucien did all the paperwork and Reyes supplied them with weapons.

"The gods . . . summoned him."

Maddox stumbled, shock momentarily blinding him. "What?" Surely he had misheard.

"The gods summoned him," Torin repeated patiently.

But the Greeks hadn't spoken to any of them since the day of Pandora's death. "What did they want? And why am I just now hearing about this?"

"One, no one knows. We were watching a movie when suddenly he straightened in his seat, expression dead, as if there were no one home. Then a few seconds later he tells us he's been summoned. None of us even had time to react—one minute Aeron was with us, the next he was gone.

"And two," Torin added with barely a pause, "I tried to tell you. You said you didn't care, remember?"

A muscle ticked below his eye. "You should have told me anyway."

"While you had barbells within your reach? Please. I'm Disease, not Stupid."

This was . . . this was . . . Maddox did not want to contemplate what this was, but could not stop the thoughts from forming. Sometimes Aeron, keeper of Wrath, lost total control of his spirit and embarked on a vengeance rampage, punishing mortals for their perceived sins. Was he now to be given a second curse for his actions, as Maddox had been all those centuries ago?

"If he does not return in the same shape he left, I will find a way to storm the heavens and slaughter every godly being I encounter."

"Your eyes are glowing bright red," Torin said. "Look, we're all confused, but Aeron will return soon and tell us what's going on."

Fair enough. He forced himself to relax. Again. "Was anyone else summoned?"

"No. Lucien is out collecting souls. Reyes is gods-know-where, probably cutting himself."

He should have known. Even though Maddox suffered unbearably each night, he pitied Reyes, who could not live a single hour without self-inflicted torture.

"What else did you have to tell me?" Maddox brushed his fingertips over the two towering columns that flanked the staircase before beginning to climb.

"I think it will be better if I show you."

Would it be worse than the announcement about Aeron? Maddox wondered, striding past the entertainment room. Their sanctuary. The chamber they'd spared no expense creating was filled with plush furniture and all the comforts a warrior could desire. There was a refrigerator crammed with special wines and beers. A pool table. A basketball hoop. A large plasma screen that was even now flashing images of three naked women in the middle of an orgy.

"I see Paris was here," he said.

Torin did not reply, but he did quicken his steps, never once glancing toward the screen.

"Never mind," Maddox muttered. Directing Torin's attention to anything carnal was unnecessarily cruel. The celibate man had to crave sex—touch—with every fiber of his being, but he would never have the option of indulging.

Even Maddox enjoyed a woman upon occasion.

His lovers were usually Paris's leftovers, those females foolish enough to try to follow Paris home, hoping to share his bed again, not knowing just how impossible such a thing was. They were always drunk with sexual arousal, a consequence of welcoming Promiscuity, so they rarely cared who

finally slid between their legs. Most times, they were all too happy to accept Maddox as a substitute—even though it was an impersonal joining, as emotionally hollow as it was physically satisfying.

It had to be that way, though. To protect their secrets, the warriors did not allow humans inside the fortress, forcing Maddox to take the women outside in the surrounding forest. He preferred them on their hands and knees, facing away from him, a swift coupling that would not rouse Violence in any way or compel him to do things that would haunt him forever and still another eternity.

Afterward, Maddox would send the females home with a warning: never return or die. It was that simple. To allow a more permanent arrangement would be foolish. He might come to care for them, and he would definitely hurt them, which would only heap even more guilt and shame upon him.

Just once, though, he would have liked to linger over a woman as Paris was able to do. He would have liked to kiss and lick her entire body; he would have liked to *drown* in her, completely losing himself, without fearing his control would snap and cause him to wound her.

Finally reaching Torin's quarters, he blocked those thoughts from his mind. Time spent wishing was time wasted, as he well knew.

> Afterward, Maddox would send the females home with a warning: never return or die. It was that simple.

He glanced at his surroundings. He'd been in this room before, but he did not remember the wall-to-wall computer system or the numerous monitors, phones and various other equipment lined throughout. Unlike Torin, Maddox eschewed most technology, for he had never quite gotten used to how quickly things seemed to change—and just how much further each new advancement seemed to pull him from the carefree warrior he'd once been. Though he would be lying if he claimed not to enjoy the convenience such gadgets provided.

Survey complete, he faced his friend. "Taking over the world?"

Unlike Torin, Maddox eschewed most technology, for he had never quite gotten used to how quickly things seemed to change—and just how much further each new advancement seemed to pull him from the carefree warrior he'd once been.

"Nope. Just watching it. It's the best way to protect us, and the best way to make a little coin." Torin plopped into a cushioned swivel chair in front of the largest screen and began typing on the keyboard. One of the blank monitors lit up, the black screen becoming intertwined with grays and whites. "All right. Here's what I wanted you to see."

Careful not to touch his friend, Maddox stepped forward. The indistinct blur gradually became thick, opaque lines. Trees, he realized. "Nice, but not something I was in dire need of viewing."

"Patience."

"Hurry," he countered.

Torin flicked him a wry glance. "Since you asked so nicely . . . I have heat sensors and cameras hidden through out our land so that I always know when someone trespasses." A few more seconds of tapping and the screen's view shifted to the right. Then there was a swift flash of red, there one moment, gone the next.

"Go back," Maddox said, tensing. He wasn't a surveillance expert. No, his skill lay in the actual killing. But even he knew what that red slash represented. Body heat.

Tap, tap, tap and the red slash once again consumed the screen.

"Human?" he asked. The silhouette was small, almost dainty.

"Definitely."

"Male or female?"

Torin shrugged. "Female, most likely. Too big to be a child, too small to be a grown man."

Hardly anyone ventured up the bleak hill at this time of night. Or even during the day. Whether it was too spooky, too gloomy or a sign of the locals' respect, Maddox didn't know. But he could count on one hand the number of deliverymen, children wanting to explore and women prowling for sex who'd braved the journey in the last year.

"One of Paris's lovers?" he asked.

"Possibly. Or . . . ."

"Or?" he prompted when his friend hesitated.

"A Hunter," Torin said grimly. "Bait, more specifically."

Maddox pressed his lips together in a harsh line. "Now I know you're teasing me."

"Think about it. Deliverymen always come with boxes and Paris's girls always race straight toward the front door. This one looks empty-handed and she's gone in circles, stopping every few minutes and doing something against the trees. Planting dynamite in an attempt to injure us, maybe. Cameras to watch us."

"If she's empty-handed—"

"Dynamite and cameras are small enough to conceal."

Maddox massaged the back of his neck. "Hunters haven't stalked or tormented us since Greece."

"Maybe their children and then their children's children have been searching for us all this time. Maybe they finally found us."

Dread suddenly curled in Maddox's stomach. First Aeron's shocking summons and now the uninvited visitor. Mere coincidence? His mind flashed back to those dark days in Greece, days of war and savagery, screams and death. Days the warriors had been more demon than man. Days a hunger for destruction had dictated their every action and human bodies had littered the streets.

Hunters had soon risen from the tortured masses, a league of mortal men intent upon destroying those who'd unleashed such evil, and a blood feud had erupted. The battles he then found himself fighting, with swords clanging and fires raging, flesh burning and peace something of lore and legend . . . .

Cunning had been the Hunters' greatest weapon, however. They had trained female Bait to seduce and distract while they swooped in for the kill. That's how they managed to murder Baden, keeper of Distrust. They had not managed to kill the demon itself, however, and it had sprung from the decimated body, crazed, demented, *warped* from the loss of its host.

Where the demon resided now, Maddox didn't know.

"The gods surely hate us," Torin said. "What better way to hurt us than to send Hunters just when we've finally carved out a somewhat peaceful life for ourselves?"

His dread intensified. "They would not wish the demons, crazed as they would surely be without us, loose upon the world. Would they?"

"Who knows why they do any of the things that they do." A statement, with no hint of a question. None of them really understood the gods, even after all these centuries. "We have to do something, Maddox."

His gaze flicked to the wall clock and he tensed. "Call Paris."

"Did. He's not answering his cell phone."

"Call—"

"Do you really think I would have disturbed you this close to midnight if there were anyone else?" Torin twisted in the seat, peering up at him with forbidding determination. "You're it."

Maddox shook his head. "Very soon, I'm going to die. I cannot be outside these walls."

"Neither can I." Something murky and dangerous shimmered in Torin's eyes, something bitter, turning the green to a poisonous emerald. "You, at least, won't obliterate the entire human race by leaving."

"Torin—"

"You're not going to win this argument, Maddox, so stop wasting time."

> Maddox shook his head. "Very soon, I'm going to die. I cannot be outside these walls."

He tangled a hand through his chin-length hair, frustration mounting. *We should leave it out there to die,* Violence proclaimed. *It*—the human.

"If it *is* a Hunter," Torin said, as if hearing his thoughts, "if it is Bait? We can't allow it to live. It must be destroyed."

"And if it's innocent and my death-curse strikes?" Maddox countered, tamping down the demon as best he could.

Guilt flashed over Torin's expression, as though every life he was responsible for taking clamored inside his conscience, begging him to rescue those he could. "That is a chance we have to take. We are not the monsters the demons would have us be."

Maddox ground his teeth together. He was not a cruel man; he was not a beast. Not heartless. He hated the waves of immorality that constantly threatened to pull him under. Hated what he did, what he was—and what he would become if he ever stopped fighting those black cravings and evil musings.

"Where is the human now?" he asked. He would venture into the night, even if it cost him terribly.

"At the Danube border."

A fifteen-minute run. He had just enough time to weapon up, find the human, usher it to shelter if it was innocent or kill it if circumstances demanded, and return to the fortress. If anything slowed him down, he could die out in the open. Anyone else foolish enough to venture onto the hill would be placed in danger. Because when the first pain hit, he would be reduced to Violence and those black cravings would consume him.

He would have no other purpose but destruction.

"If I don't return by midnight, have one of the others search for my body, as well as Lucien's and Reyes's." Both Death and Pain came to him each night at midnight, no matter where Maddox was. Pain rendered the blows and Death escorted his soul to hell, where it would remain, tortured by fire and demons almost as loathsome as Violence, until morning.

Unfortunately, Maddox could not guarantee his friends' safety out in the open. He might hurt them before they completed their tasks. And if he hurt them, the anguish he would feel would be second only to the agony of the death-curse that visited him every night.

> Anyone else foolish enough to venture onto the hill would be placed in danger. Because when the first pain hit, he would be reduced to Violence and those black cravings would consume him.

"Promise me," he said.

Eyes bleak, Torin nodded. "Be careful, my friend."

He stalked out of the room, his movements rushed. Before he made it halfway down the hall, however, Torin called, "Maddox. You might want to look at this."

Backtracking, he experienced another slap of dread. What now? Could anything be worse? When he stood in front of the monitors once more, he arched a brow at Torin, a silent command to hurry.

Torin motioned to the screen with a tilt of his chin. "Looks like there are four more of them. All male . . . or Amazons. They weren't there earlier."

"Damn this." Maddox studied the four new slashes of red, each one bigger than the last. They were closing in on the little one. Yes, things could indeed be worse. "I'll take care of them," he said. "All of them." Once more he leapt into motion, his pace more clipped.

He reached his bedroom and headed straight to the closet, bypassing the bed, the only piece of furniture in the room. He'd destroyed his dresser, mirror and chairs in one fit of violence or another.

At one time, he'd been foolish enough to fill the space with tranquil indoor waterfalls, plants, crosses, anything to promote peace and soothe raw nerves. None of it had worked and all had been smashed beyond repair in a matter of minutes as the demon overtook him. Since then he'd opted for what Paris called a minimalist look.

The only reason he still had a bed was because it was made of metal and Reyes needed *something* to chain him to as midnight drew near. They kept an abundant supply of mattresses, sheets, chains and metal headboards in one of the bedrooms next door. Just in case.

Hurry! Quickly, he jerked a black t-shirt over his head, pulled on a pair of boots and strapped blades to his wrists, waist and ankles. No guns. He and Violence were in agreement about one thing— enemies needed to die up close and personal.

If any of the humans in the forest proved to be Hunters or Bait, nothing could save them now. ❖

YOU CAN'T TAKE IT WITH YOU IF YOU'RE NOT GOING ANYWHERE.

Forever is a long, long time—especially when it comes to financial planning. Forever-Mutual, the bank designed with the immortal family in mind, can help you grow your nest egg over the centuries. Our investment specialists will keep your money secure for eons to come.

Our experts have thousands of years of hands-on experience. Come in (after hours) and talk to one about our:

- 500-year CDs
- Refinancing packages for the castle, cave, or keep
- Eternal portfolio management
- Life-sized safe deposit boxes for secure and confidential valuables storage

...and much more.

You'll rest easy with ForeverMutual

Fiction Preview!
The First Two Chapters of
Gena Showalter's
Forthcoming Blockbuster . . .

The Darkest Seduction

We are so happy to bring readers of *DTU* this exclusive: a brand new, never-before-shared excerpt from *The Darkest Seduction*, Book 9 in Gena's bestselling Lords of the Underworld series, to be published in March 2012. This sizzling-hot page-turner features Paris, your favorite Lord—immortal warrior, dark seducer, and the keeper of the Demon of Promiscuity. Though no woman can resist his legendary appeal, he is the most tortured of the Lords of the Underworld, for he wants what he can never have: the god king's most prized slave. Will Paris at last find a way to save her?

CHAPTER ONE

Paris tossed back three fingers of Glenlivet and signaled the bartender. He wanted an entire hand and by gods, he'd have it. Except soon after the single malt was poured, he realized an entire hand wasn't going to cut it either. Fury and frustration were living entities inside him, frothing and bubbling despite his recent fighting.

"Leave the bottle," he said when the bartender made a move to help someone else. Hell, suddenly Paris doubted every drop of alcohol in a ten-mile radius would do the trick, but whatever. Desperate times.

"Sure, sure. Anything you say." Shirtless Boy Wonder released the bottle and at last beat feet.

What? He looked *that* dangerous? Please. He'd washed off the blood, hadn't he? Wait. *Hadn't he?* He looked down. Fan-freaking-tastic. He hadn't. Crimson streaked him from head to toe.

Whatever.

Call him back, Promiscuity, the Demon trapped inside Paris said. *I want him.*

We don't always get what we want, do we? he replied. No one knew that better than him.

A growl sounded in Paris's head as he downed the second offering and quickly chased it with a third. Both scorched so good he enjoyed a fourth. The potent alcohol razed his chest, burned holes in his abdomen and flooded his veins. *Nice.*

And yet, his emotions remained as dark as ever, the edges of that bone-deep fury and frustration unsmoothed. His inability to save a not-so-innocent woman he should hate, *did* hate, at least a little, but one he also hungered to have, body and soul, drove him onward, a constant whip against his flank.

"If I asked you to leave, would you?" a monotone voice said from beside him.

He didn't have to look to know that Zacharel, warrior Angel extraordinaire and infamous Demon-assassin, had just joined him. They'd met a few weeks ago, when the feathered ax-man had come to Buda to off his friend Amun. Had Zach actually succeeded, two crystal blades would have been drilling into his spine at that very moment.

I want him, the Demon said.

Screw you. Once upon a time, the Demon had talked to Paris nonstop. Then he'd stopped, merely urging Paris to take this person or that person. Now, the talking had started up again and it was freaking annoying.

"Well?" the Angel prompted.

"No, I wouldn't leave, but I'd damn sure want to know why you give a shit."

"I do not."

True story. Zacharel didn't care about anything. "So get lost."

As Paris nursed a fifth whiskey, he studied the smoke-stained mirror in front of him, covertly panning the area behind him. Bejeweled chandeliers hung from the ceiling. The walls were rose-colored marble veined with glittering ebony, the floor a sparkling stretch of crushed diamonds.

Throughout the room, men and women talked and laughed. They were immortals, like him. From minor gods and goddesses to fallen Angels trying to work their way back into their saintly fold. Yeah. *Good luck with that in a bar. Morons.* Anyway. There was probably a Demon or two sprinkled among the masses, but Paris couldn't tell for sure.

Demons were sneaky little bastards. They could skulk around in their own scales, proudly showcasing their horns, claws, wings and tails—and being decapitated by warrior Angels like Zach. Or they could possess someone else's body and skulk around in *their* skin.

Paris had thousands of years of experience with the latter.

"I will leave, as you so . . . succinctly suggested," Zacharel said. "After you answer another question for me."

"All right." Something else Paris knew from experience: Angels were freakishly stubborn. Better to hear the guy out, otherwise he'd find himself with a tail. "Shoot."

He turned, facing the dark-haired stunner with eyes the color of jade, and sucked in a breath.

Never ceased to amaze him how sexually magnetic these celestial beings were. No matter their gender—or how mind-numbingly dull their personalities were—they drew and held your attention.

Majestic wings arched over the Angel's broad shoulders, a turbulent fall of winter snowflakes with rivers of gold winding and curling throughout. Dressed in a long white robe, which was customary for his kind, he should have looked prissy as hell. Instead, he looked like the Grim Reaper's evil twin. Emotionless, as frigid as the Arctic, and ready to kill.

"Do you wish to die?" Zacharel asked.

Okay. Definitely ready to kill. "What do you think?" he asked, because honestly, he didn't know the answer anymore. For centuries he'd fought to live, but now, now he constantly threw himself into the fire and waited to be burned.

Unflinching, the Angel held his gaze. "I think you want one particular woman more than you want anything else. Even death . . . even life."

He pressed his tongue to the roof of his mouth. One woman in particular—the not-so-innocent one.

> Unflinching, the Angel held his gaze. "I think you want one particular woman more than you want anything else. Even death . . . even life."

Her name was Sienna Blackstone. Once a Hunter—that irritating army of humans who sought to rid the world of all Demonic influence—and always his enemy. Then, fleetingly, his lover. Then, dead, gone. *Then,* brought back from the grave, her soul merged with the Demon of Wrath. Now, she was out there. Somewhere. And she was suffering. Cronus, the newly reinstated king of the gods, had enslaved her, and now that he'd lost control of her, he thought he could torture her into submission. Why he was so desperate to use her, Paris didn't know.

What he did know: no matter what the reason, no matter what was necessary, he would save her.

Already he'd stepped over the line between right

and wrong—and there was no fooling himself into thinking the line had merely been blurred. He'd known his actions were reprehensible, and he'd stepped over anyway. He'd killed, callously. Seduced, methodically. Lied, cheated . . . betrayed. All of which he would do again. And again.

He might dislike the things Sienna had done to him, and yeah, as he'd already admitted, part of him might even hate the woman herself, but even she did not deserve such cruel, vicious—eternal—punishment.

Once he found her, he would set her free. From Cronus . . . from himself. And maybe, in the process, he would even free himself from his obsession with her. As some of the girls he'd slept with over the years liked to say: fingers crossed.

"So I want her," he ended up saying to the Angel. Sienna was not up for discussion. "BFD."

"I will pretend I know what that means. As for you, I think that, despite your own desires, your Demon wants anything with a pulse."

"Sometimes a pulse isn't even a requirement," he muttered, and damn if that wasn't the truth. Sex, as he called his dark companion, wanted anyone and everyone—but only once. With the exception of Sienna, the bastard would not allow Paris to grow hard for the same woman twice. And why he could have Sienna again? No clue. "But again, so?"

"I think, even though you crave this particular woman, you slept with your friend Strider's future wife. He is possessed by the Demon of Defeat, and your actions made his courtship of the female very difficult."

"Hey, now. You're entering dangerous territory." Not that Paris had anything to apologize for.

The one-nighter had happened weeks before Strider and Kaia hooked up. Or even thought about hooking up. Therefore, Paris had done nothing wrong. Technically. And yet, he now knew what Kaia looked like naked, and Strider knew that he knew, and that meant all three of them knew Sex tossed out naked images of the girl every time they were together. A consequence Paris loathed, but couldn't stop.

Zacharel's head tilted to the side. "I mean only to point out that you have clearly moved on to other conquests, and that you are not . . . discriminating in your choices. Which makes me wonder why you still pursue Sienna."

Because I'm hungry, Sex snapped.

Because Sienna had been Paris's only shot at monogamy. Because he'd inadvertently aided in her death. Because he'd felt like he'd lost *everything* when she died. "You're annoying," he snarled, mentally high-fiving his Demon. Sometimes they actually got along. "I'm done talking to you."

"I think you feel guilty about every heart you break, every dream of happily-ever-after you crush, every bit of self-loathing you encourage when your partners realize how easily you overcame their reservations," the Angel continued, unperturbed. "I also think you are overindulged and pathetic, and you have no business crying about your problems."

"I've never cried," Paris gritted out, slamming his glass on the counter with so much force the bar split down the center and the cup shattered. Blood welled from slices in his palm, but the sting was minimal. "And you know what? *I* think you're seconds away from finding pieces of your body scattered in all the corners of this bar."

Then, while he's down, we can have him!

And sometimes he and his Demon didn't get along. *Zip it, Sex.*

Those eyes of jade narrowed to tiny slits. "I think you hope to save this woman, and that is a good thing. I think you mean to keep her, and that is not. No matter how intensely you crave her, no matter that she might be your only chance at forever, your Demon will eventually ruin her, cause her to—"

"Enough!" If they continued on this path, his fury and frustration would rise up and consume him. He would lose sight of tonight's goal. He would attack. "I'm not going to keep her." He would. He *so* would. If she'd have him, but hell, she wouldn't have him.

"Here," the bartender said, Johnny-on-the-spot with a clean rag he thrust in Paris's direction.

I want—

I said zip it! "Thanks," Paris forced himself to reply with an even tone. He fisted the material, applying pressure to the slivers of torn tissue before anyone could scent him and his oh, so special pheromones.

"Any, uh, time." The man, one of the fallen judging by the thick wing-like scars on his back that glared at Paris from the mirror's reflection, cleaned up the mess. That his gaze failed to remain on Paris, that he still projected fear, was odd.

Usually Sex exuded an intoxicating scent that was unforgivably arousing to everyone around him. Both males and females would find themselves hopping the train to Pleasure Town, uncaring where they were or who they were with. And though that would have been an especially craptastic outcome tonight—considering Paris was in the heavens, surrounded by warriors of equal strength, and operating under a time crunch—the lack stunned him. Especially considering Sex wanted to do everyone who approached them.

"Would this particular woman like the man you have become?" Zacharel asked, drawing him back to the present.

> **Usually Sex exuded an intoxicating scent that was unforgivably arousing to everyone around him.**

Snorting, he shoved his free hand back and forth through his hair. "She didn't like who I was."

"And yet you still rush to save her."

Yeah. He was as big a moron as the fallen who frequented this place. Whatever. He *knew.* "Look, I don't answer to you. I don't have to explain myself."

Zacharel leaned into him and whispered, "I think, if you continue on this destructive path, you will lose everything you've come to love."

"Is that a threat?" Paris jerked away to fist the collar of the Angel's robe. "Go ahead and try something, winger. See what—"

Air. He was fisting and yelling at air. *Damn it!* Little growls sprang from him as he lowered his arm to his side.

"Uh, who were you talking to?" the bartender asked, faux casual as he cleaned the counter.

So, only Paris had seen Zacharel. "No one." If an Angel didn't want to be seen, an Angel wouldn't be seen. Not even by his immortal brethren. Which made Paris wonder. Was Zacharel still here? Or had he materialized somewhere else? And what the hell had that little visit been about?

Once he'd gotten himself under control, Paris dropped the rag and turned the rest of the way to face the crowd. Several warriors were scowling in his direction, dangerously close to ruining the room's elegance with the blood they were tempting Paris to splatter.

Continue on his destructive path? With pleasure. Paris flipped off the men, but though their scowls deepened, they didn't charge him. Too bad. Another fight might have calmed him.

He massaged the back of his neck, forcing thoughts of Zacharel and his threat into hiding. He was here for Viola, the minor goddess of the afterlife as well as the keeper of the Demon of Narcissism. She should have popped in already.

Maybe she'd heard he was coming and bailed. After all, even though they'd never met, the girl had to hate his guts.

He and his buds had once stolen and opened Pandora's box, unleashing the evil from inside. As punishment, they were cursed to host the Demons they'd released within themselves. Unfortunately, there'd been more Demons than naughty boys and girls to contain them, the box had disappeared in the chaos and the leftover evil spirits had needed homes. Who better for the gods to select than the unlucky, unable-to-run inmates of Tartarus, Olympus's immortal prison?

So Paris was partly responsible for Viola's dark side, seeing how she'd been one of those unlucky prisoners. Not entirely responsible, though, considering the girl was a criminal. A criminal once considered dangerous enough to lock away for all eternity. What crime she'd committed, though, he didn't care. She could laugh while slashing him to ribbons, if that's what she enjoyed, as long as she gave up the information he craved.

He. Was. Close. So damn close to saving Sienna.

Weeks ago, he'd snuck into Cronus's secret harem and seduced one of the god king's concubines, trading sex for information. A trade that had paid off. He now knew where Sienna was being held. The Realm of Blood and Shadows, a homage to two of the realms found in hell itself, though supposedly worse than both of them combined. To enter was to die, blah, blah, blah, whatever.

Paris could find the realm on his own, no problem. He'd gotten very good at bribing his way between earth, heaven, and each of the godly dominions. But finding it would do him no good if he couldn't freaking find *Sienna.* She was a soul without a body—a soul he couldn't sense in any way. Only those who communed with the dead could see, hear, or touch her. But rumor was Viola knew a trick that rendered the ability unnecessary.

According to the Hunters he'd slain just this morning, Viola came here every Friday night to hustle gods at pool and rave about her awesomeness over a few beers. Apparently, they'd been watching her, intent on nabbing her and forcing her to join their army. So, in a way, she kinda owed him.

Where the hell is she? he wondered again, searching for the telltale long blond hair, eyes the color of cinnamon, and a killer body that could—

Appear in a puff of white smoke.

There, in front of the bar's only entrance, stood a luscious woman with long blond hair and eyes the color of, what? Cinnamon. Paris straightened, his nerve-endings zinging with anticipation. Just like that. Prey located. Target acquired.

CHAPTER TWO

I want her, Sex said as Paris studied the goddess.

Of course you do, he replied dryly.

The tendrils of smoke that had marked Viola's appearance now curled away from her, thinning out to reveal a slinky black dress. The thick straps on her shoulders veed to frame heavy cleavage before dipping past her pierced navel. The micro-mini skirt stopped just below the hem of her panties.

Was she even wearing panties?

Yeah, Sex wanted to find out as much as he wanted to climb on top of her. Bastard was practically drooling inside Paris's head. Was definitely panting.

Paris yawned. He'd been with gorgeous women, ugly women, and everything in between. One lesson he'd quickly learned: beauty could hide a beast, and a beast could hide a beauty.

Sienna was the perfect example. She considered herself plain, and maybe once he would have agreed. But from the beginning, there'd been something tantalizing about her. Something that drew him, held him captive. Now, any time he pictured her, he saw a flawless gem with no equal.

Viola flipped the length of her silky hair over one sun-kissed shoulder and scouted her surroundings. Men openly gaped. Women tried to hide their scowls. She paused on Paris, looked him up and down, her lids narrowing, and then, shockingly, she dismissed him and finished her visual sweep.

The last time he'd endured so many dismissals, he'd met Sienna shortly thereafter. Could that mean . . . what if . . . . His anticipation intensified until his bones vibrated. He would get his answers —*tonight*—no matter what was required.

He closed the distance between them, schooling his features to reveal only admiration as he went over his plan. Charm first, if he could actually remember how to be charming. Force second, and yeah, he definitely remembered how to go that route.

Ignoring his approach, Viola bent down and slid a glittery pink phone out from inside her black leather boot. Her nimble fingers flew over its tiny keyboard. He frowned.

"What are you doing?" As an opener, the question blew. As did his accusing tone. Still. If she thought to summon help, someone to fight him, or hell, a Hunter to kill him, she'd soon find herself his hostage as well as his informant.

"I'm Screeching. That's the godly version of Twittering or Tweeting or whatever you lower beings want to call it," she said without glancing up. "I've got over seven bazillion followers."

Okay. Not what he'd expected. He'd spent a lot of time with humans, and knew they enjoyed sharing their every inane thought with the world.

A goddess who did so—that was new. "What are you telling them?" Was Cronus among the seven "bazillion?" Was Galen, the head honcho of the Hunters?

"I maybe might be kinda sorta telling them all about you." A grin lifted the corners of her plump, red lips. "'Lord of Sex is filthy and looking to score. I'm not interested, but should I help him rack up the points with someone else?' Send." She typed as she spoke. And after pressing *send,* she focused on him. "I'll let you know when the results come in. Until then, is there anything else you want to know about me before I walk away and ignore you?"

Lord of Sex. So, she knew who he was, *what* he was, but she wasn't running, wasn't tossing insults and wasn't screaming for his execution. A great start. "Yes, there is, and it's a private matter very important to me." Subtext: don't godsdamn Screech.

"Ohhh. I love private, important matters that I can tell the world about. I'm listening."

Despite her claim to tattle, there was no more typing. Good. "I want to see the dead. How do I make that happen?" Short and sweet.

> Lord of Sex. So, she knew who he was, *what* he was, but she wasn't running, wasn't tossing insults and wasn't screaming for his execution.

She blinked, and he noticed that her pink, glittery lashes matched her phone. "Let me tell you what I just heard. Talk, talk, talk, *I.* Talk, talk, talk *I.* Well, what about *me?*"

His jaw clenched. There was being charming, and there was being a sucker. He wasn't a sucker. Well, not all the time. "I'll tell you what about you. You can see the dead. Now you're going to teach *me* how to see them." An order she would do well to heed.

Her nose wrinkled. "Why do you care about seeing souls? They're hideous creatures. Just hideous. Oh, oh, wait." Clap, clap, jump, jump, twirl. "I've already figured it out because I'm highly intelligent and mysteries are my bitch. You want to see your slain human lover."

Instantly his fury flashed to the surface, hot, so hot. He didn't like anyone speaking of Sienna in any fashion. Not Zacharel, and certainly not this minor goddess. Sienna was his to protect, even in that capacity. "I—"

"Tsk, tsk. No need to confirm my genius assumption." Viola patted his cheek, all syrupy sweetness. "Especially since I can't help you."

"Can't or won't?" There was a big difference. The first he could do nothing about. The second he could change, and if she pushed him, she would discover the lengths he was willing to go to do just that.

"Won't. See ya." She practically skipped to the back of the bar, her perfect ass swaying, the heels of her boots clicking.

Incensed, he followed her, shoving aside anyone who got in his way. Grunts, groans, and growls abounded, the predators in the crowd taking exception to his brute-force tactics. No one attempted to stop him, however.

"How do you know who I am?" he demanded the moment he reached Viola. They'd start there and work their way to the mind-changing.

She performed another twirl, making a production of it, as if she were a model at the end of a runway. He was a tall man used to towering over women, but Viola was a tiny fluff of five feet nothing and he *dwarfed* her.

Sienna, on the other hand, was just the right height.

"I know everything there is to know about the Lords of the Underworld," Viola said. "I made the entire horde of you my business when I escaped Tartarus and learned you were responsible for my condition."

She blamed him for the Demon she was stuck with, then. Despised him as he'd first assumed. And she smelled of roses, he realized, the gentle scent suddenly clinging to his sinuses, very nearly drowning him in a warm sense of peace. Inadvertently or on purpose? Either way, his fury and frustration proved far more potent and quickly chased the calm away.

"Wow, that's a dark scowl. And not a very good look for you, I must say," she added, catching a glimpse of her coral-painted fingernails and studying them in the light.

Touch her.

He tuned out his Demon and decided he'd give the charm/sucker thing one more shot. Because, honestly? He had yet to intimidate her in any way. If this next shot failed, he would unleash his beast full-force. And he wasn't talking about Sex. There was darkness inside him now. So much darkness.

He'd opened himself up to it. Just a fraction at first, like cracking a window. But the funny thing was, once you welcomed a breeze, there was no stopping what came next. A wind, a storm, thunder and lightning, until you could no longer reach the window to close it—and didn't want to.

Lie, cheat, betray, Paris thought. He leaned down, softening his expression, letting his Demon's desires seep through his pores. Letting his blood heat, the musky scent of arousal drifting from him, as sultry as champagne, as heady as chocolate.

"Viola, sweetness. Talk to me. Tell me what I wish to know." His tone was a verbal caress.

Inside his head, Sex jumped up and down, up and down, impatient, demanding that Paris coax the goddess into stripping, now, now, *now.* Resisting wasn't difficult.

"I meant to thank you," she went on, as if he'd never spoken. "But then halfway to Budapest, I forgot all about you. I'm sure you understand." She fluffed her hair, looking away from him as she waved to someone at her right. "So, anyway, now that you're here, thanks. And now that that's taken care of, you'll have to—argh! Who the hell put a mirror there?"

Paris thought he caught a glimpse of undiluted rage in her expression, but couldn't be sure. A heartbeat later, she appeared rapturous as she studied her reflection.

"Look at me." She angled one way, posed, then another. Posed again. *"I'm gorgeous."*

"Viola." Minutes passed, but she never stopped admiring herself. She even blew herself a kiss. Fine. They'd do this the other way. "I can make you beg for my touch, Viola. In front of everyone. And believe me, you *will* beg. You will cry, but relief will never be yours."

Several more minutes ticked by, but she never offered a reply.

Fury . . .

Frustration . . .

Darkness . . . rising . . . he wanted to attack, to hurt, to kill.

He inhaled, held, held . . . an infusion of roses . . . released the breath. Okay. Good. Both emotion-bombs fizzled before detonation, calming him, allowing him to refocus on the goddess, who was still preening, unconcerned with anything around her.

Why would she ignore his threat? Why would she stop Screeching to her followers? Unless . . . she might not be able to help herself, he realized suddenly. As he knew very well, all of Pandora's Demons came with a major flaw. This could be hers. She was Narcissism, after all. A lover of self.

Testing his theory, he stepped in front of her, blocking her view of the mirror. Her entire body stiffened. Her gaze darted left and right, as if searching for interlopers who might have tried to harm her while she'd been incapacitated. No one had approached, and the tension drained from her. She breathed easier.

"I will *gut* the culprit!" she whispered fiercely.

Bingo. Her flaw, and one she reviled.

"Concentrate on me, Viola." He gripped her by the shoulders, squeezing harder than he'd intended and shaking her until her gaze met his. "Tell me what I want to know, and you'll walk away from this."

Still not the least bit intimidated, she shrugged off his hold. "Let's see what my worshippers have to say sooner rather than later, shall we?" She lifted her phone and read the screen. "Four hundred and eighty-five votes for *help him by giving him my number.* Two hundred and seven votes for *are you stupid, climb him like a mountain,* and one hundred and twenty-three votes for *he's mine, bitch, walk away.*" She looked up at him, another smile taking root. "They have spoken. Yes, I will tell you about the souls."

Urgency overrode his relief. "Tell. Now."

"Hey, you. Demon scum." The harsh voice rang out behind him.

Aaand, one of the guys Paris had bumped into earlier was finally acting out. He ground his molars. His hands returned to the goddess's shoulders. "Viola. Tell me."

"Get your hands off my female!"

Or not. He arched a brow at the goddess, the need for violence rising yet again. *Restrain yourself,* common sense counseled. Victory was finally within reach. "A friend of yours?"

"I have no friends." Graceful fingers reached up and hooked several tendrils of her hair behind her ear. "Only admirers."

"I'm talking to you, Demon."

That need was rising . . . higher and higher . . . a thick black cloud that would not dissipate until blood ran in rivers at his feet. "If you want this admirer to survive, flash us out of here." Popping from one location to another with only a thought always made him sick, but sick was better than distracted.

"I don't," she said. "Want him to survive, that is."

"Are you listening to me, Demon?" The tone was harsher now, and far more determined. "Move away from her and face me. Or are you a coward?"

The cloud enveloped his mind, a single thought consuming him. The male was an obstacle in his path, blocking him from Sienna, and obstacles were to be eliminated. Always.

Another small voice of reason whispered through him, beacons of gold in the midnight of his soul. Zacharel . . . current path . . . destruction . . . .

"Goddess, look at yourself in the mirror," the male commanded. "I don't want you to see what I do to the Demon."

Even as a curse tore from her mouth, she obeyed, as if she couldn't help but do so. And like that, she was once again utterly enraptured with herself, pinkie waving and blowing kisses.

The whisper was destroyed. Death, inevitable. Paris pivoted on his heels to glare at his opponent. Soon, blood would flow. ❖

RECOVERGIRL

BEFORE   AFTER

THEY'LL NEVER KNOW YOUR SECRET!

Keep that special guy you're dating under wraps until you're ready to reveal him to the world with RecoverGirl's specially formulated concealing products. Eye bags, scaley abrasions, singeing— and those tell-tale bite marks—vanish instantly and stay hidden all day!

RG
QUEEN OF
THE NIGHT
CONCEALER
Oil-free
Noncomedogenic

RG
BURNIN'
LOVE
COVERUP
Oil-free
Noncomedogenic

RG
UNDEAD
UNDEREYE
CORRECTOR
Oil-free
Noncomedogenic

Your bundle of joy is waiting at **W.O.L.F.**

You met your vampire and fell in love, and now it's "bloodily ever after" time. There's just one thing missing from your perfect future—the patter of furry little feet.

That's where **W.O.L.F.** comes in. We are a fully licensed and accredited adoption agency, matching qualified Vampire families with adorable little Werewolf babies from the litters born every day.

Come visit the furry little creatures just waiting for your love and attention. We don't think you'll be able to leave without a few of the precious pups.

Call **1-666-WEREPUP** to make an appointment today!

W.O.L.F.
Wanted: One Loving Family

Learnin' the Lingo

A Few Terms and Definitions to Help You Understand Your Paranormal Man and Stay Away from His Dark Side!

Alpha: The leader or "top dog" of a Werewolf pack. Dating an Alpha sounds exciting, but keep in mind: It's hard for you to be the Alpha in the relationship if he's the leader of the pack!

aPod: Portable listening device favored by Angels (tends to feature New Age music and Gregorian chants—with a bit of Bieber and Bublé for variety).

AVC: American Vampire Council. They make life—and death—decisions for younger Vamplings, as well as approve or disapprove potential human turnings.

Bait: Females that the Hunters use to lure the Lords of the Underworld to their doom.

BHGF: Best Human Guy Friend. We all need a few of these, no matter how obsessed we are with immortals.

Hatchling: Derogatory name for Dragons. Though they were once hatched, today's Dragon-Shifters are born in their human form. They reach full dragon maturity within the first twenty years of life.

Hunters: The army of humans who hope to destroy the Lords of the Underworld.

Immortal: Any creature of the undead, such as Vampires, Shape-Shifters, Zombies, Angels, Dragons, and Demons. Another definition might be, the hottest guys in the universe!

Immortox: Detoxing one's self of an immortal, often necessary to get over a breakup. This is an "inside and out" kind of thing . . . because, once they get under your skin, they are as hard to remove as a Bloody Mary from a white shag rug.

LG: Slang for "living girl"—us! And we *do* like to live, don't we?

Mindtreat: Thinking naughty thoughts for a mind-reading creature—such as an Angel— to enjoy. So . . . if you want to blow your Angel's mind, try thinking, *I'm not wearing any panties. That's right, cutie . . . nothing under here but skin . . . .*

MM: Mortal Man. You may think you've moved beyond them, but give these guys a break—they make great friends, brothers, and fathers, right?

Myth-Information:
Misconceptions and legends about the undead, usually created by the immortals themselves (especially those who work secretly in Hollywood), meant to confuse humans about the powers and qualities of the immortals.

Undead: Slang for *immortal*. Some people get off on the term, others prefer to put it more delicately—any way you slice it, these guys we love aren't quite alive—but they are far from dead!

Vampling: A newly turned Vampire. Be very careful how you sling this term around . . . while we LGs love to be complimented on our youthfulness, Vampires can be a little touchy about being treated as if they are children of 150 once they've reached their maturity. (Our "21" is their "300," if you were wondering.)

WIA: Worldwide Immortal Association. When different species of immortals have problems, the WIA can issue punishments, decree ownership rights, and more. Plus, they throw a hell of an annual convention!

Winger: Slang for *Angels*. (They don't mind this one too much.)

Were: Slang for *Werewolf-Shifters*. But you probably figured that out. ❖

Zombie Jack's Turn

The Guy's-Eye View of Life with Your Immortal

Every month, we ask our favorite "sensitive" Zombie to weigh in on some of the things that surprise or confuse us about the immortals we love. This month, ZJ turns his attention to a few issues that keep us LGs tossing and turning when we should be catching up on our beauty sleep.

My Vamp says he is devoted to me for eternity—so why do his fangs come out every time a pretty girl in a boatneck sweater strolls by?

I wish I had a bag of chips for every time I've been asked about the Vamps' notoriously roving red eyes. The short answer is, they can't help it. Think about it this way. Your mouth waters and you stare every time you spot a delicious 72-ounce steak searing to rare perfection, right? Maybe you even start to breathe heavily as the smoke rises from the thick, juicy . . . wait. Okay, maybe that's just me. Sorry. *Your* mouth waters and you stare every time you spot a moist, creamy chocolate cake, right? Well, that's how it is for Vamps and veins. They see and they crave. Do you always devour that cake? No. You think about the calories and the fat grams and reach for the rice cake. Again, same with Vamps. (Not that I'm comparing you to a stale rice cake.)

You have to remember that your bloodthirsty beloved has heightened senses—and that makes for some powerful lovemaking—but it has a downside. He can smell that pretty wench even before he spots her, and one whiff of the warm elixir flowing through her veins brings those incisors out of hiding. It's not that he doesn't prize you above all others—

it's just that he is endlessly thirsty. But don't worry. If your immortal is in a committed relationship with you, he can look but he won't touch.

Or rather, he *shouldn't* touch. Just as with human men, you have a right to expect fidelity. That means "fangs off—you're with me now." If his appetite takes him elsewhere, it might be time for you to find a new immortal. May I recommend a Zombie? We're pretty damn faithful, and with the right lotion applied liberally over our flesh every day (a sensual experience in itself), our skin looks glitter-in-the-sun amazing.

ZJ, I hope you don't take this the wrong way, but I am really curious. I am currently in a long-term relationship with a heavenly Angel and couldn't be happier. In the past, I've dated a few Vampires, a Dragon, and even a Demon (okay, I admit I had a rather extended "experimental" phase)—but I've never dated a Zombie and never wanted to. Honestly, when I see a beautiful LG make a play for some goofy Zombie in a bar or the local 7-Eleven, I just don't understand it. What do Zombies have to offer? What in heaven or hell am I missing out on?

I take no offense at the question, don't worry. In fact, one of the qualities we Zs are proud of is our unflappability. It takes a lot to rile up our tempers (but . . . I guess I should add that when we *do* lose it, limbs start flying—and not just our own).

Because I don't want to come off as self-serving, I decided to ask some of my Zombie friends' LG girlfriends what it is they find so appealing about us. And what was the quality most often cited? Nope, not our superior video-gaming skills or our way with a steak and a barbecue—it was our loyalty. We Zombies are pretty monogamous. (Okay, part of it is laziness and the inability to run as fast or pounce as hard as our Demon, Vamp, or Were counterparts—but still.) Once we find a nice girl with whom we can share the complete DVD box set of *Battlestar Galactica*, we tend to stick around. Not even our eyes wander—and that's not nothing. Check out the previous question.

We're easygoing, easy-to-please, and just love to "nest." Unlike our Demon friends, we're perfectly content to cuddle when you're not in the mood, and we're happy to accompany you to your parents' house for dinner, though, come to think of it, that hardly ever comes up. And . . . you know how some guys (ahem, Mr. Angel) tend to be competitive with you about who has the more impressive job title, knows more foreign languages, bakes the best soufflé, whatever? Well, that ain't us. We are proud of our LG girlfriends' accomplishments, supportive of their hard work, hobbies, and skills and happy to be the beneficiary of all of the good things they bring home to us while we wait contentedly on the couch.

Are you starting to get the picture? For thrills and chills—or peerless virtue—go a different way. We won't hold it against you. But rest assured, there are lots of LGs out there who wouldn't trade their Zombies for all of the Angels on the head of a pin. So . . . when you get ready for a little more experimentation, hit me, care of the magazine! I'm just dying to find the right LG to share my hammock this summer.

ZJ, help! I'm just out of a toxic relationship with a Demon, and he really did a number on my self-esteem. I don't know how many times I heard: *You're no fun.*

Why can't you keep up? Let's have a three-way. **After the breakup, I was too miserable to even get out of bed. And when my girlfriends finally did drag me out on the town, I couldn't even talk to an immortal, let alone entertain the possibility of falling for one. Maybe understanding why I fell for the wrong guy will help me move on—can you enlighten me? Will I ever be able to trust myself, or another undead guy?**

Oh, my pretty friend, I'm sorry you got hurt. Every time I see a Demon waltz off with a beautiful LG on his arm (or, more likely, one on *each* arm), I can't help thinking "bad for the immortals." It is 90 percent the fault of the Demons that we undead are feared and shunned (and even hunted) by humans—especially human females. How can we ever hope for complete equality—including marriage equality and the right to serve in the military—as long as there are Demons out there making us all look like untrustworthy, lecherous fiends?

In all fairness, I certainly understand the appeal they have. I mean—they all look like European fashion models who can bench press buses, and they dress like them, too. They have killer smiles, know all of the best clubs and restaurants (and can sail right past the bouncers—because the bouncers jump out of the way). And in the bedroom . . . well . . . that's where they leave the rest of us in the dust, or so I'm told. I'm not trying to make you feel bad here, but I want you to see that it isn't your fault you fell for a Demon. It happens to the best LGs, so don't beat yourself up about it.

As far as "moving on" is concerned, take your time. Start by accepting a few innocent dates with Angels or, uh, Zombies, who are more than happy to take things s-l-o-w-l-y (see the question above). And as you start to feel a little bit daring and in need of more stimulation—though, I'm telling you, Zombies can be stimulating—find yourself a beautifully furry Werewolf and go for a trial romp. The exercise will help clear that Demon out of your thoughts, and the feel of his strong, hairy arms around you as he lifts you onto his back might just stir those feelings of safety and security you crave. Who knows? You might find yourself waking up contented in his den, happily in love again—this time, with a guy who only goes out on a howl once a month at the most, and always comes home with something for dinner. ❖

Angel vs. Demon

As you've probably guessed, we at *DTU* are nothing if not open-minded. That's why we like to offer several perspectives on the issues that concern our LG readers. Check out Angel's answers to your thorny questions—then read what Demon has to say. We leave it to you to decide whose advice to follow, but we suggest considering both and finding your own happy medium. After all, with an Angel on one shoulder and a Devil on the other, you can't go too far wrong, right? Each immortal has his gifts. (At the magazine, for example, we leave the travel arrangements to Angel, while Demon takes care of security. But that's enough about us . . . this column is for *you*.)

Dear DTU,

My boyfriend is a Werewolf, and one of the things I love about him is that he adores eating as much as I do. (Okay, he'd just as soon hunt his food down and kill it first—but there's still plenty of overlap in our tastes.) The problem is—his hours. As you can imagine, he's a "night person." By the time he comes home from a prowl and showers the leaves and twigs out of his fur, I'm gearing up to go to work. I'm thinking about scheduling a romantic sunrise hook-up at the gourmet donut shop near where we live. They make the sweet treats right in front of you. Even better, you get to eat them by candle-light. What do you think? Will this revive our passion for each other?

Signed,
Sweet Tooth

 Angel says . . .

Heavenly thinking, my sweet! Instead of complaining about something you can't change (his proclivity for night rambling), you are working around his natural drives to come up with a thoughtful, romantic compromise. I do have a suggestion, though. Why don't you buy those donuts "to go," and eat them outside, picnic-style. That way, you'll be indulging his affinity for the outdoors while you both enjoy a beautiful sunrise. Just be sure to dispose of your trash in the proper receptacles (and recycle!) You wouldn't want to rile up Mother Nature when she's provided you with such a divine backdrop. And don't lose track of time—you wouldn't want to be late for work!

 Demon says . . .

You know that saying, "Man does not live by bread alone?" Well neither does woman. Or wolf. There's more than one way to satisfy your appetites, and in my opinion, you are focusing on the wrong one. Instead of devising a breakfast rendezvous, how about taking a day off and clocking a few laps around the bedroom? You need to stay in shape if you want to keep up with your Were (and look tasty in those little track shorts he likes). Donuts won't help you in that regard—but a vigorous afternoon game of Catch Me will. And if you are worried about missing a day at the office, remember that other saying: "All work and no play makes Sweet Tooth a very dull LG indeed."

To behave or misbehave? Our experts say there are two sides to everything.

Dear DTU,

My Zombie and I have been talking about taking a vacation together. (Well, I've been talking about it. He usually just nods and goes back to watching baseball on the flat-screen.) The problem is . . . where to go? The beach is out since he burns so easily and hates the water, and he's definitely not the hiking or skiing type. He'd be happy lying on a shady hammock in the country, but my allergies would turn me into a sniffly, sneezy mess. He once suggested we attend a comic book convention—spare me! There must be something we can enjoy together besides a Vince Vaughn movie and a large buttered popcorn.

Signed,
Stymied

Angel says . . .

First of all, bless you—I have a soft spot for LGs who love Zombies. It takes a special girl to appreciate the appeal of those easygoing (if not physically prepossessing) fellows. You will certainly be rewarded for your warm-heartedness in the afterlife. As for your vacation dilemma, here's an idea: How about surprising him with a trip to his favorite baseball team's spring training camp?

Pack sunscreen and his official team cap and jersey so he won't burn, and see how his eyes light up as he watches his heroes round the bases and swat at fastballs. If you get a little bored, you can always slip away for an hour or two and shop the local outlet malls for a divine little number to wear to dinner. Before he realizes you're gone, you'll be back with hotdogs and beer for two! (May I add that you cannot go wrong if the team you visit happens to come from Los Angeles?)

Demon says . . .

Did you hear the joke about the Zombie hockey game? There was a face off in the corner! Hahahahaha . . . that one never gets old. But I kid. I think it's sweet that you and the Big Z want to share some leisure time together. If you were *my* LG, we'd be jetting off to Amsterdam, where anything goes, everything is legal, and girlfriends come in two-packs—but my pick for the two of you would be a nice booze cruise around the Caribbean. Nothing to do all day but hang out at the all-you-can-eat buffet and all-you-can-drink pool bar, visit the gaming tables or video arcade, catch a lounge act—and if you're really feeling energetic, play a game of

shuffleboard or bingo. And he never has to get in the water! The evening is sure to bring more indulgences (did I mention all-you-can-drink?) followed by a return to your stateroom for some sexy fun before you pass out. Sounds like Zombie heaven to me.

Dear DTU,

I really owe my Vampire boyfriend—he has been taking such good care of me since we met, always bringing me flowers and other romantic gifts and flying me to exotic surprise destinations. Of course it is hard to know what to get the eternal man who has everything (in spite of *DTU*'s helpful gift guides). What do you think of this idea? I take him to a planetarium show featuring the sun, solar eclipses, sunspots, etc. He hasn't seen genuine sunlight since he made the change and I figure he might be missing it. Will this cheer him up—or am I just rubbing salt in the puncture wounds?

Signed,
Light of His Life

Angel says . . .

I literally have tears in my eyes at your thoughtfulness. That Vamp is a lucky guy to have such a creative and caring

LGfriend! I am sure he will delight in the experience and feel just that much closer to heaven (and you) because of it. If you want to take your idea one step further, and your Vamp is on the pale end of the spectrum, why don't you follow up your planetarium visit with a session of indoor tanning for two at a local salon catering to mixed couples? The new technology designed to turn undead skin to his once-live hue without burning is spectacular—I've tried it myself and am the envy of my fellow wingers. Enjoy!

Demon says . . .

Oh, please. I like everything about the above except the planetarium and Angel's tanning idea. Which means— change everything! Look, your guy knew what he was signing up for when he became a Vamp, so 86 the sun and help him revel in his dark side. The only ball of fire that matters is the one that ignites when you touch him. If you really think he is missing the light, stay home, slip into something super-sexy, and start some fireworks of your own. That is the only gift your guy (or any guy) really wants. Well . . . that and a cold Bludweiser afterwards. And maybe a couple of great seats to a Kiss concert. Trust me.

Dear DTU,

I've been seeing a Dragon-Shifter for several months. Everything's been wonderful but I've been hiding a little secret. I am terribly afraid of heights! Lately, he's started asking me when I will visit his mountain lair, instead of always insisting we stay at my place. The only way to get there is on his back—and it is on a mountaintop overlooking an abyss! The thought of the flight puts me in a tailspin, and once we get there, I'll be clinging to the walls in terror. I'm afraid he'll leave me if he finds out about my phobia. Are we incompatible, or is it worth trying to ground him? We get along so well in other ways.

Signed,
Two Feet Firmly Planted

Angel says . . .

Fear of flying . . . that has never crossed my mind! Of course, we Angels tend to glide gracefully through the upper atmosphere (on long trips, I like to listen to Sarah McLachlan or Enya on my aPod), while my Dragon friends do a fair amount of diving, swooping, and screeching—so I can imagine it might be a little bit daunting. Here's the thing, though. A good relationship can't thrive without total honesty. You must sit down with him, look him straight in his fiery eyes, and tell him the truth. If he loves you, he will understand completely and agree to take things slowly. Maybe you'd be willing to start with a low pass around the neighborhood, then gradually increase the height and distance until you feel one

hundred percent comfortable in the upper atmosphere. Before you take off, come up with a "safe word" that means "bring me back to earth immediately." That way, you never have to worry about getting carried away—until you are completely ready, that is. Take it from a veteran wingman. you'll be glad you faced your fears and soared.

Demon says . . .

Big surprise—I disagree with Angel again. All of this talk about flying makes me a little queasy myself. We Demons like our hooves on the ground whenever possible—under the ground, even—so I'm sympathetic to your need for an airsickness bag. Why not just bag the Dragon? They aren't the only creatures on the farm, you know. We Demons know how to throw a party for two—and it doesn't involve clinging to the side of a mountain. If it's his fire you are addicted to, no problem. I can show you a place where there are plenty of flames to go around, and you won't have to go airborne to get there. My advice? If you have to change in order to be with someone, walk away instead and stay your own sweet, sexy self. Relationships are about fun with a healthy dose of lust, and shouldn't involve all this work, sacrifice, and commitment. Why don't you people see that? ❖

COMING NEXT MONTH:
Angel and Demon offer their unique perspectives on one-night stands, what to do if you catch him cheating, and how to react when he forgets your anniversary—again.

Run with the Wolves in Our Go-Everywhere Gear!

ON SALE FOR FALL:
Our classic Muck Boots—perfect
for a tramp through Transylvania!

Keeping up with that special guy means stocking up on just the right clothing and accessories. Whether you are winter camping with your Werewolf, soaring through the heavens with the Angel of your dreams, or accompanying your Zombie on a midnight raid of the 7-Eleven, we've got the gear to get you there in style—warm, dry, splatter-proof, wrinkle free—and oh-so-stylish.

L.L.Brain

Real-Life
Lords of the Underworld
Bare All!

The winners of our best contest ever step forward to claim their prizes! Will you be the one to share a fantasy vacation with one of these blazing hot immortal wannabes?

Long ago, twelve immortal warriors, each more dangerously seductive than the last, stole and opened Pandora's box, unleashing the evil from within. Now, as punishment, these sexy heartthrobs carry that evil within themselves. Violence, Death, Pain, Doubt, Wrath, Lies, Secrets, Defeat, Promiscuity, Disaster, Misery, and Disease—that's a lot of baggage. And yet, we LGs (and many immortal women as well) are obsessed with them. What is the secret of their endless appeal? Could it be that we want to comfort and heal their tragic spirits—or is it just those rockin' hot bodies we crave? Probably a little of each.

For all of their flaws and burdens, their appeal to the fairer sex makes the Lords the envy of every mortal guy on the planet. So we thought it would be fun to come up with a way that mere mortals could compete with these demigods on their own terms—or at least try to. We asked human hunks to send in their photos, along with a few lines telling us why they think they'd make the perfect honorary Lord of the Underworld. Boy, did we get a big response! Clearly, there are a lot of earthly gents who think they've got the stuff of legend. (We suspect that some of you ladies had a hand in talking your guy pals into responding—or maybe you even snapped or swiped a photo when they weren't looking and responded for them? That's okay—we'll never know for sure.)

Anyway, we had a ball here at *DTU* reading all the entries and got into a few arguments over our favorites. But we finally settled on our Top Twelve—and each one will walk away with a fab trip for two to the lost city of Atlantis, complete with land, sea, and airfare and an all-access pass. Here's what the top contenders had to say:

John Brody is
Maddox

Hair: Brown with golden highlights

Eyes: Gray

Height: 6'1"

Distinctive characteristics: Has a twin brother and multiple scars on his knuckles

"Possessed by the Demon of Violence, Maddox has a fierce temper, even fiercer fists, and he's not afraid of a good brawl. As a cage fighter, neither am I. I throw down with the best of them.

"Another thing we have in common? Maddox is nothing but gentle with his woman. Maybe that's because he regrets the terrible things he did upon his possession, or maybe it's because he knows a good thing when he sees it. Like him, I'm actually a real sweet guy underneath the muscles. I go for blonds who are strong and self-sacrificing, and when I meet the right one, I know it'll be magic."

Hair: Black

Eyes: Brown

Height: 6'

Distinctive characteristics: Frequent rug burns

"Lucien is the keeper of Death, tasked with escorting souls to heaven or hell. As a pilot, I escort humans all over the globe. Mile-High Club? Yeah, I'm a member. A founding member.

"What I love most about Lucien is his ability to take charge of any situation—and anyone. Add in the fact that he hooked up with a feisty goddess known for her mischievous nature, and oh, baby, is he living the high life. While I don't need a goddess to rev my engine, I'm all about the naughty fun to be had with a woman lacking inhibitions. So if you're a lovely lady who enjoys adventure, you can soar through the clouds with me anytime."

Alfred Graham is
Lucien

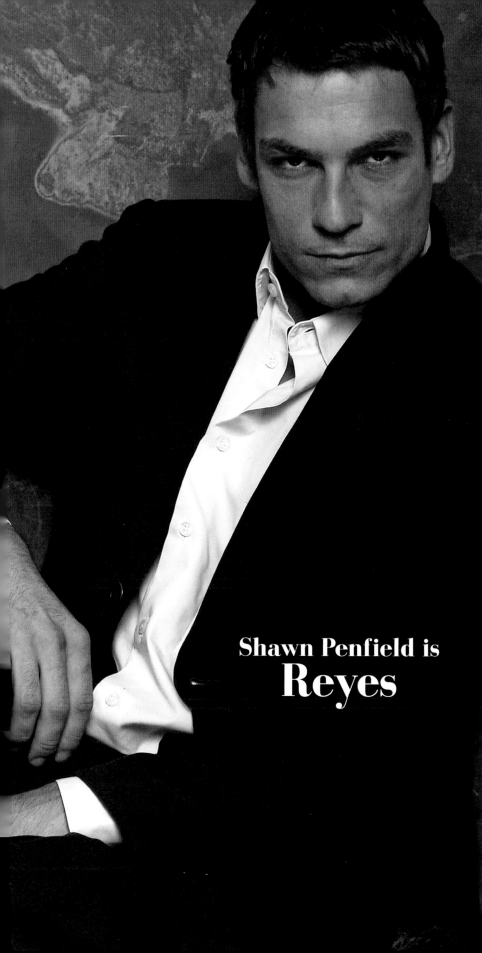

Hair: Black

Eyes: Black

Height: 6'3"

Distinctive characteristics: Cleft in chin, heart of gold

"Reyes is the keeper of Pain, and he has to cut himself to feed his Demon. I get it. When I was a teenager, I used to cut myself to ease my own tormented soul. I've since learned to deal with my problems in a more constructive way: I'm a therapist.

"Shockingly enough, however, what most connects me to Reyes isn't our affinity with blades. When he fell in love with his beautiful blond, he immediately put her on a pedestal, treating her like the treasure she is. When I fall in love, I plan to do the same. Of course, I'm hoping my girl won't be wearing any panties. And yes, she can call me Dr. Love."

Shawn Penfield is
Reyes

Ralph Marshall is
Sabin

Hair: Dark brown

Eyes: Brown

Height: 6'3"

Distinctive characteristics: Prosthetic left foot (lost in battle)

"Sabin is the keeper of Doubt, and I'm an Army Ranger. He can talk anyone out of their faith in anything, true, but like me, he's a warrior who kicks ass and doesn't care about names. And okay, maybe he enjoys torturing his enemies a little too much, but there's one thing we both know beyond *any* doubt: we're willing to die to protect the ones we love.

"Actually, there's something else we have in common, and that is a straight-up sense of crazy for redheads—and the fierce tempers that come with them. What's more, I love that, no matter the situation, he treats his woman like an equal. Well, except in bed, where he lets her take charge. Yeah, there's little wonder why he's my hero. "

Liam Barton is
Aeron

Hair: Dark blond

Eyes: Green

Height: 5'10"

Distinctive characteristics: Both legs are tattooed with dragons (both ice and fire)

"Aeron is the keeper of Wrath, a badass who punishes those who sin. I'm a miner who battles a little hell myself every time I enter the caverns. My job may not be glamorous, but I sure can pick out the diamonds.

"I wasn't surprised when Aeron mated with an actual Angel who fell from heaven just to save him—or when he introduced her to a wild side she hadn't known she possessed. Of course, now Aeron might want to punish *me* for *my* sin. Envy. He's got the total package: naughty and nice. I want that. Bad."

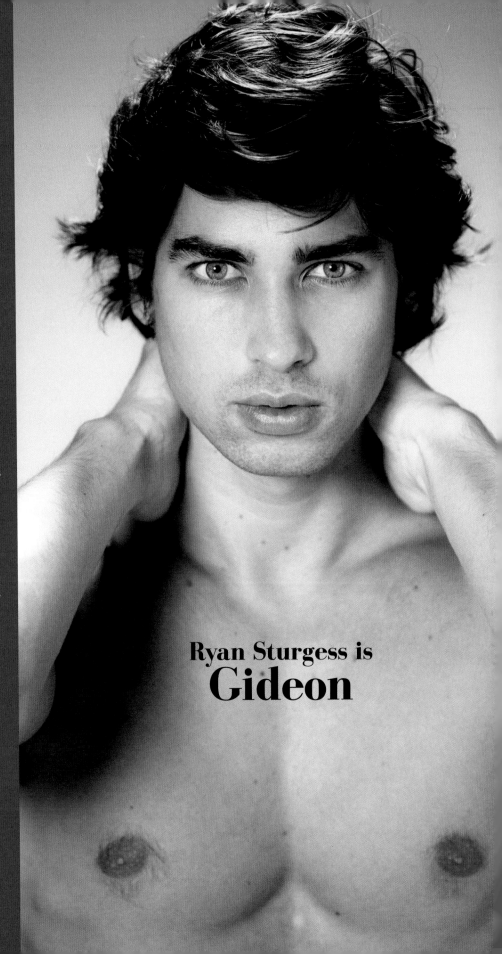

Hair: Black

Eyes: Blue

Height: 5'11"

Distinctive characteristics: Numerous piercings—but none that you can see

"Gideon is the keeper of Lies, and he can't speak a word of truth without experiencing intense pain. Me? I'm a sexy, single, impressively endowed billionaire looking for love—with you. And that's the God's honest truth.

"The thing I admire most about Gideon, though, is that he paired himself with the keeper of Nightmares, a dark-haired female with a red-hot body, a tortured past, and a shocking vulnerability that makes a man want to, well, cuddle her forever. After pleasuring the ever-loving hell out of her, that is."

Ryan Sturgess is
Gideon

Hair: Bald (on purpose!)

Eyes: Brown

Height: 6'

Distinctive characteristics: Tribal tattoo on left bicep

"Amun is the keeper of Secrets and he can't speak without revealing things we're better off not knowing. Therefore, he doesn't speak; he signs. His loyalty to his friends is unparalleled, and his deep capacity for love is astounding.

"As a former CIA operative, I know what it means to keep secrets—and to get in bed with the enemy in order to get my job done. The fact that Amun fell in love with a woman playing for Team Hater, someone he'd inadvertently hurt in the past, and then romanced her so tenderly that he *earned* her forgiveness, puts him at the top of my Most Admired list. I want to be just like him."

Joshua St. Cloud is
Amun

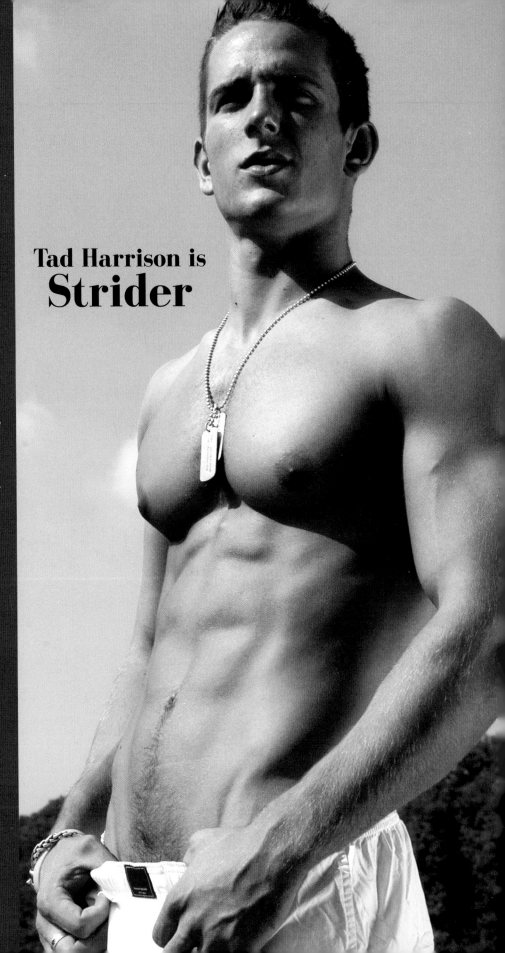

Hair: Dark blond

Eyes: Hazel

Height: 6'1"

Distinctive characteristics: Eagle tattooed on back, and while he will strip down to nothing, he'll always wear his tags

"Strider is the keeper of Defeat. If he loses a challenge, he's down for the count. That, I understand. As a Navy SEAL, I'm all about the V in victory. Giving up isn't ever an option.

"When it came to winning his woman's heart, he did whatever it took to succeed. Fight her enemies? Check. Cheer her on while she did a little fighting of her own? Check. Make love to her until she begged for mercy? Double check. And that's exactly what a woman can expect from me."

Tad Harrison is
Strider

Jason Brody is
Paris

Hair: Brown (with fewer high-lights than his brother)

Eyes: Gray

Height: 6'1"

Distinctive characteristics: Has a twin brother, hates to shave, and has a six-inch scar on his right thigh

"Paris is the keeper of Promiscuity. He has to sleep with a new person every night or he weakens and dies. I've had my fair share of lovers, and I've learned my way around the female body. But what I really want to do is learn my way around *yours*.

"Don't get me wrong. I'm not in the market for a one-nighter. I'm actively looking for my true love. That doesn't make me different from Paris; that actually makes me more *like* him. He's addicted to one particular female—the one that got away—and he's moving heaven and earth to find her. This is something I understand. When I find my one and only, I'll have to have her and only her."

<Editor's Note: We had twice as many entries for Paris as all of the other Lords combined!>

Hair: Dirty blond

Eyes: Blue-green

Height: 6'3"

Distinctive characteristics:
X tattooed over heart

"Kane is the keeper of
Disaster, and he's known
(and accidentally caused)
countless tragedies. As a
surgeon, I know the beauty
of overcoming hardship. Not
to mention the fact that I'm
very good with my hands.

"While Kane avoids women
to protect them, I know that
deep down he craves female
companionship. He wants
to love and be loved. All I
can say is, I know the feeling.
We're protectors by nature.
We just can't help ourselves."

Shelton Heltfield is
Kane

Clark Adams is
Cameo

Hair: Brown

Eyes: Brown

Height: 5'11"

Distinctive characteristics: Heart-shaped birthmark on left hip

"Cameo is the keeper of Misery, and yeah, she's the only female warrior. Well, I'm here to tell you that I'm all man (as you can see), but I'm not afraid of my sensitive side. My mission in life will be dispelling your misery and making you smile, in bed and out. But mostly in.

"The reason that I identify with Cameo more than the other warriors is that, despite her constant bombardment of sadness and pain, she manages to find (and savor) moments of utter joy. Anyone with the strength to do that is someone worth imitating. And getting into bed. (I'm just sayin'.)"

<Editor's Note: We got fewer entries for Cameo than any other. In fact, this was the only one!>

Dirk Laughlin is
Torin

Hair: Brown

Eyes: Brown

Height: 6'4"

Distinctive characteristics: Multiple scars from multiple injuries

"Torin is the keeper of Disease, and he can't touch anyone skin-to-skin without starting a plague. Which means, he hasn't touched anyone—or *been* touched— in centuries. His solidarity has made him an honorable yet dirty-minded virgin! What he wants more than anything is an eternity of passion, though at this point I'm sure he's will-ing to settle for a single night.

"I'm a professional football player and part-time racecar enthusiast—so it might surprise you to learn that I am saving myself for that one-and-only woman. It's been tough, sure—I mean . . . look at me. Don't get me wrong. I've dated a lot of great girls and experimented plenty, but the big prize will go to the woman who's in it for the long haul—and willing to take that ride in the slow lane, where we can enjoy the scenery for life!" ❖

If it's love, it must be…
deKAY.

He knows what makes your heart skip a beat: that tiny box with a black ribbon, of course! Whether it's a special rosary from your dreamy Angel or a diamond-studded flea collar (so handy!) from the Werewolf you cherish, a gift from deKay Jewelers means he cares enough to mate for life.

Fit Forever!

Even Shape-Shifters need an occasional shape-up. . . . These killer workouts for two will keep you both fit for eternity—and give you energy to burn.

Your Vamp's tattooed chest is to die for! Your Demon's got killer guns—and they might even be loaded! How about the way your Angel can fly from New York to the Vatican without breaking a sweat? (Well . . . Angels don't sweat, they glow—but you know what we mean.) Ever wonder how your paranormal stud-muffin stays in such great shape century after century, in spite of devouring whatever catches his fancy and burning the midnight oil seven nights out of seven?

The same way you do, dearest LGs! Sorry to disappoint you, but the afterlife doesn't include any magic fitness formulas (other than the fact that their bodies heal twice as quickly as yours do, so no need to break out the Ben-Gay).

That's right. In spite of what he might tell you, your perfect, hard-bodied immortal doesn't stay that way without a little effort. And when he gets lazy, it can all go to hell pretty quickly. So, if your Zombie has been gorging himself on stale pizza and takeout, or your Vamp is in a blood-coma and feeling sluggish, or your Dragon has been having more fun burning villages than *feeling* the burn—we've got some new tricks for you. These one-plus-one workouts are designed to shape you both up— and bring you closer together in the process. What are you waiting for? Set the alarm for 7:00 a.m. (or sundown, as the case may be) and coax him out of the lair for some joint workouts. We promise you—far from sapping his energy for sweet, sweaty love—a little exercise will rev you both up for an even hotter bedroom workout. (Ooh, did we really say that? Don't tell Angel!) And by the way, did you know that studies have shown that LGs burn twice as many calories making love to an immortal? Just another reason to love them!

Six Great Workouts for You and Your Immortal

1 Hit the obstacle course with your Vampire.

There is nothing a Vamp likes more than showing off his speed, strength, and ability to overcome any obstacle—so bring him to Vamp Camp for an hour-long ab blasting, blood-racing workout. The obstacle course at the world-famous Vamp boot camp is specially designed to offer both you and your man a killer workout. Wear comfortable shoes and clothing, and make sure you are well-hydrated (and your Vamp is well-bloodrated) before attacking the patented course of tree hurdles, rock scampering, mountaineering, and triple long jumping, culminating in a final speed-of-light sprint to the finish line. It's a fun and blood-racing way to stay fit. To help you rebalance your electrolytes post-workout, his-and-hers snack packs are available for you: Type AB for him, bananas and trail mix for you.

Check out www.vampcamp4u.com for schedules and a location in your realm.

2 Run with the Wolves.

Your furry Were is a pack animal (and the last time he ran a trail alone, he scared the local neighborhood watch). Ergo, group workouts are the way to go here. Luckily for the wolf-minded LG, these guys are just fine with pretty strangers tagging along—if you can keep up, that is. Wolf workouts begin with a 10-mile run through the woods, followed by a 2-mile doggie paddle in the nearest body of water (a designated swimming pool will suffice if there are no lakes nearby). After cardio, the Weres head for their local Fit Forever gym for some heavy lifting. Think bus presses and truck squats—but don't worry about keeping up there. These gyms always keep free weights on hand for mortals and cubs. While you are doing your reps, you will love watching your guy and his pack toss around farm equipment and monster-truck tires. Be prepared for loud woofing and barking, and an occasional impromptu brawl on the wrestling mat.

3 Fly with your Dragon.

If you have always been just a teeny bit envious of your Dragon's power of flight, here's a way to join the fun without being a passenger— and get a great workout in the process. Visit Dragonfly's Flying Trapeze, and while he's working his wings and abs, you'll be flexing your own muscles and experiencing the thrill of solo flight at the same time. Under the tutelage of Dragon-trainer-to-the-stars Dragonfly Smoketrail, you'll be spinning through the air with the greatest of ease in no time, while your Dragon swoops alongside to catch you if you slip. (No need for a net under these enchanting circumstances!) Once you've mastered the fundamentals, the two of you can move on to the intermediate course, where you will learn to launch yourself into your fiery friend's arms in midair—what could be more thrilling?

For more information contact Dragonfly@flying-trapeze.com.

4 Go on a long-distance stalk with your Zombie.

If you love a Zombie, then you know that it is just about impossible to get him to do anything he doesn't want to do. But, while exercise is not at the top of any Zom's to-do list, there is one outdoor activity that every one of them loves as much as junk food and the couch: stalking! You've seen them out there on chilly nights, arms stretched forward for balance, eyes glazed over with joy, legs lurching forward at a steady .25 miles per hour. Suggest a long stalk and your dream dude will be out of the house before you can say *burger and fries*. As you grunt and lurch along beside him, follow his form for a great upper-arm workout and enough lunges to transform your backside into a boulder. Be sure to bring snack bites for both of you for stamina (Rot Pockets for him, Power Bars for you), and watch out for overflowing trashcans, which might make him lose his focus. After a couple of hours (and a couple of blocks), you'll both be feeling the burn.

5 Take a splash with your Angel.

It may be news to you, but your heavenly immortal craves the serenity of a water work-out. Some Angels say that a long swim reminds them of gliding through the cool clouds of lower Paradise, while others crave liquid exercise as the perfect time to stare up at the heavens while doing the winged backstroke. Join your Angel for a watery workout, and while he is enjoying his fitness face-up, you can freestyle alongside him for an all-over fat-burn. Afterwards, help him by blow-drying his weary, feathery appendages (on low, to avoid wing singe, please!).

6 Try your hand at martial arts with your Demon.

Very few things about living with a Demon are easy—but an exception is getting him to exercise. These mighty dudes have energy to burn, and a conscientious Demon knows that he (and the world) is safest when he works out every day—just as a form of anger management. Not surprisingly, Demons thrive on aggressive forms of exercise such as wrestling, boxing, and other types of combat martial arts. Lucky for you, these hands-on workouts are designed for two—and provide a vigorous and healthy workout (as long as you manage to avoid getting tossed through a wall). Our favorite martial arts club, Demoniacs, caters to "mixed" couples and provides an undead referee for every match to ensure that your Demon doesn't get dangerous. Sign up for a ten-week starter course designed to introduce you and your devil man to the finer points of kicking, jabbing, and pinning. Both fire and ice Demons are welcome, and part of each afternoon is devoted to mixed-Demon death match demos for your LG entertainment.

Visit: www.MMA4demoniacs.net to sign up for a starter course guaranteed to send you home sweaty, sleepy, and sore. ❖

Happy, Healthy Afterlife!

You are what you eat (or what eats you)—so it pays to think before you feed.

It's hard enough for us health- and body-conscious LGs to watch what we eat under normal circumstances—but when things turn *para*normal (i.e., you've hooked up with one of them), things get really tricky. You know the old saying, "When you're dating a Vampire, you're eating for two." Well, that's just for starters. What do you do when your favorite Zombie whips you up a batch of his specialty, Brains Bolognese—and you know it will send your cholesterol through the roof? How do you pack a picnic when your Werefriend wants nothing more than a rabbit's foot (and not on his keychain)?

Dating outside your species is a matter of finding enjoyable compromises in all areas, and that includes healthy eating. Maybe you both like sashimi and beef carpaccio—it's a start—but there are plenty of other delectable things you can cook up when sitting down to a meal for two. We've concocted a few things sure to satisfy your "plus-un" while keeping both of you energized and fit for an afterlifetime of romps, frolics, rituals, and howls.

As our fiendish friends like to say, "Bone appetit!"

Six Healthy Meals That'll Tame Your Savage Beast

1. Beef up dinner with your Vamp.

You enjoy a good steak paired with red wine—and he enjoys watching you snack on the bloody thing, while he swirls a glass of vintage type O. Treat yourself to a portion of grass-fed filet mignon and marinate it in red wine and coarsely ground pepper. Grill it as rare as you can stand it (make sure he is standing nearby as the juices sizzle in the pan and that bloody aroma wafts through the kitchen). Pair it with a mash-up of roasted tomatoes for even more crimson on the plate, and—voilà!—a perfect dinner of protein and veggies for you, and a great show for your non-eater. Enjoy each bite provocatively, allowing the meat and tomato juices to slither down your chin. The effect will be so appetizing for him that you are sure to be dessert!

2. Have a hoagie picnic with your Zombie.

Who doesn't enjoy a good picnic? There's something about eating outdoors that makes everything taste better. For your Zom, that usually means raiding the nearest trash can for leftovers or picking the baloney out of a kid's lunchbox when he isn't looking—so he'll really appreciate a fresh and tasty outdoor meal prepared with love by his favorite LG. And trust us when we tell you that a good overstuffed sub will win his heart every time. Sounds unhealthy, you say? Think again. Our heart-healthy hoagie starts with a whole wheat roll. Slather it with Dijon mustard, then sneak in as much tomato, lettuce, and onion as you can get away with. Add some lean smoked turkey or roast beef, add a side of crunchy carrot sticks instead of chips (he'll only pout for a minute), and wash it all down with lemony iced tea. After lunch, coax him off the blanket by bringing out the Frisbee . . . he'll be breaking a sweat without complaining, we guarantee.

3. Prowl the poultry aisle with your Werewolf.

That sexy wolfman of yours has never met a bird he didn't chase. Instead of being annoyed by that quirk, put it to use and create some mealtime fun! Grab the biggest, baddest live chicken you can find from a nearby local farm and turn it loose for your Were to catch. It's great exercise for him, and the experience will make him feel more emotionally connected to the cooking and eating experience. Enjoy couples time as you de-feather and clean the bird together. And while it is roasting, serve your guy the organs as a little appetizer. When it's done, remove the skin (where most of the fat is) before you serve the chicken, and add a few roasted potatoes and a salad. Howlingly delicious—and healthy, too!

4. Flip something fluffy for your Angel.

If you are lucky enough to be dating a heavenly Angel, you know that he's a morning creature—and breakfast is what puts a spring in his wings. This morning meal will make you feel as virtuous as he is! Whip up eight egg whites with a dash of nonfat milk until they are as frothy as feathers—then pour the mixture into a pan sprayed with Pam and cook up a fluffy omelet for two. For a heavenly (and super-healthy) variation, sauté some fresh spinach and/or fresh sliced mushrooms before adding the egg mixture. Pair your omelet with a toasted whole wheat English muffin lightly coated with almond butter and homemade strawberry jam. Serve with a glass of fresh-squeezed orange juice, and both of you will float through the rest of the day.

5. Indulge in friendly fire with your Dragon.

Dragons don't care what they eat as long as it's fiery, and this can cause them health problems aplenty. All of that barbecue, fire-roasted this and coal-charred that, can lead to heartburn or worse. But a savvy LG can satisfy his taste for burnt and spicy flesh by adding a few drops of Tabasco and turning down the flames in favor of slowly oven-roasting his favorite meat. (Add a few vegetables while you're at it.) Our shape-shifty friends also love boiling-hot soup, so try making him a steaming bowl of chicken pho loaded with bok choy, grass herbs, and some more of that tangy Tabasco. (Go easy on your portion—you don't have the flame retardant tongue your beast has been blessed with!) Hot cider spiced with cinnamon, nutmeg, and cloves makes even his beverage hot and spicy. As long as you watch your own intake (and keep some Pepto-Dismal handy just in case), you should be in for a hot night!

6. Enjoy pizza night with your Demon.

You probably don't have a wood-fired oven at home, so you'll have to go out for this one—but it will be worth the trip just to see the look on your Demon's face when he stares into the hellmouth of the oven at your local pizzeria and gazes on the charred perfection of that bubbling pizza. (Be sure to grab a table near the kitchen, so he can catch a glimpse of "home" any time he wants.) He'll be in hell and you'll be in heaven as you bite into the crispy crust and feel the blood-red sauce ooze down your chins. And, hey—in moderation, it's healthy! A thin crust topped by protein-rich cheese, fresh tomatoes, and maybe some vegetables offers a balanced meal when paired with a salad. Take home the leftovers instead of wolfing them down—and call it hell warmed over! ❖

Te-Killa
Demonically Delicious.

When it's party time, there's only one sure way to light his fire:
a kiss and a cocktail made from genuine Te-Killa.

Te-Killarita

**1 (6 ounce) can frozen
limeade concentrate**

6 fluid ounces Te-Killa

2 fluid ounces triple sec

Fill a blender with crushed ice. Pour in limeade concentrate,
Te-Killa, and triple sec. Blend until smooth. Pour into
glasses and watch the sparks fly!

Angel in the Kitchen

Diabolically Delicious Dishes to Tame His Raging Appetite

The Barechested Contessa is the author of The Bone Appétit Cookbook.

The Contessa is the Executive Chef of Otherworldly in the heart of New Orleans, as well as a member of the Research Chefs Association specializing in paranormal cuisine. Her motto: If he doesn't like it, he's not paranormal, he's abnormal. *Her inventive and immortal soul-satisfying recipes have kept many a stressed out LG from taking meal planning too seriously. It's food . . . it's supposed to be fun!*

Have you ever said, "I like to create menus to die for—except he's already dead. Or . . . not really alive. I'm not even sure what he eats. Or if!" Serving that first meal to your paranormal man is no reason to freak out and growl. You have to start somewhere, so here are a few of my favorite surefire (pun intended) creature-pleasers. Not one of them takes more than an hour to make, and every ingredient can be found in your local food market or ancient apothecary shop.

devilishly rich midnight soul-fflé

After a long night of partying and corrupting souls, all your Demon wants to do is stuff his face with the perfect late-night snack and hit the sheets . . . with you. Here's a dish sure to delight your devilish fiend and earn you a diabolically satisfying reward!

¼ cup grated cheese (Swiss or Cheddar)*

2½ tbsp butter

¾ cup hot milk

3 tbsp flour

½ tsp salt (plus a pinch)

⅛ tsp pepper

3 large eggs

3 additional egg whites

¼ tsp cream of tartar

pinch of optional spices for flavor (mustard powder, nutmeg, or cayenne pepper)

¾ cup chopped ham or other cooked meat (optional)

2 tbsp crushed Hell weed (not for humans)

*If no meat is added, use a full cup of cheese

■ Preheat oven to 350 degrees.

■ You will need a baking dish with sides about 5 inches tall for the soul-fflé and another baking dish filled with water to hold the soul-fflé dish. The water will need to be at least half way up the sides of the soul-fflé pan.

■ Spray the pan with nonstick cooking spray, or if you are feeling decadent, spread butter generously on the bottom and sides of the baking dish. This will make unmolding the soul-fflé easier. Then coat the bottom and sides with the cheese, conserving a quarter of it for later use.

■ Melt butter over moderate heat, stir in the flour and cook for about two minutes. DO NOT BROWN. Remove from heat and add milk. Beat with a wire whisk. Return to heat and bring to a boil while stirring. Remove from heat again after about 30 seconds and beat in salt and pepper. Set aside.

■ In a clean bowl, break 3 eggs, one at a time, separating the yolks. Add the yolks to your hot flour and milk base and beat.

■ With a mixer, beat all six egg whites until they turn foamy. Add a pinch of salt and cream of tartar and any other spices you prefer. For your Demon, add the crushed Hell weed here (the spicy heat is to die for, meaning it will kill you!) Beat at high speed until eggs form stiff peaks.

■ Stir a quarter of the egg whites into hot flour and milk base. Add the remaining cheese and meat. Fold the remaining egg whites in quickly. DO NOT BEAT. You do not want your egg whites to collapse. Once combined, scoop everything into your soul-fflé pan.

■ Cook for 1 hour and 15 minutes. Soul-fflé will be done when top is brown. You can do a fancy presentation and unmold the soul-fflé onto a decorative plate, or if you're too hungry to wait, eat straight from the pan after allowing food to cool.

howlriffic cassoulet

This hearty casserole has enough meat to thrill the hungriest wolf on the block. Another plus—once he gets a whiff, not even a full moon will keep him away.

½ pound thickly sliced bacon

1 pound of lamb or duck (or a pound of dark meat chicken)

1 pound of smoked chorizo (or a pound fully cooked Italian sausage links)

1 dollop of butter (optional or as needed)

4 tsps minced garlic

1 large red onion, chopped

2 cups chicken stock (not broth)

¼ cup cognac (optional)

6 Roma tomatoes, seeded and diced (or use a can with added oregano for more zip)

2 tbsp tomato paste

4 carrots, sliced in thin rounds

1 cup fresh or frozen green beans

¼ cup fresh chopped parsley

1 tbsp dried thyme

½ tsp poultry seasoning

⅛ tsp of crumbled bay leaf

salt and pepper to taste

1 can of great northern beans

1 package of refrigerated crescent rolls

1 cup moon blooms, diced

■ Preheat oven to 325 degrees.

■ Cut the meats into bite-sized chunks, but do not mix them.

■ Brown the bacon in a cast iron enamel pot first, leaving the grease in the pan. (If you don't have a cast iron pot, use a nonstick skillet.) Brown the other meats in the grease, adding butter or olive oil if needed. Remove meat from pan and set aside.

■ Add the garlic and onion to the grease still left in pan and cook until soft (about 4 minutes).

■ Stir in all other ingredients and meat. If you used a non-stick skillet, transfer mixture to an oven safe baking dish.

■ Add cognac and enough stock to cover the mixture. Cover and cook for 1 hour and 20 minutes, checking periodically to see if you need more stock. Carefully remove pan from oven and remove the top so it can cool a bit. Remove the dough from the package, unroll it, and place it carefully on top of the cassoulet in one layer. (It's okay to stretch it a bit to cover, but try not to handle too much.) Return the pan to the oven uncovered for 10–15 minutes, until it browns and puffs up.

■ Remove from oven and spread the moon blooms over the entire dish. This colorful flower with edible petals can only be found on nights of the full moon, but most groceries now carry bags in the fruit section. He'll be howling for more!

gourmet sloppy zomboes

While every Zombie loves Pringle-encrusted fish fingers, it might be time to mix things up a bit! One bite of this zesty favorite, and your couch potato will be drooling for more.

3 pounds of lean ground beef

1 medium onion, chopped

1 red pepper, seeded and chopped (optional)

3 tsp minced garlic

¼ cup packed brown sugar (more if you prefer a sweeter flavor)

2 tbsp red wine vinegar

2 tbsp Worcestershire sauce

1 6-oz can of tomato paste

2 15-oz cans of tomato sauce

1 bag Ruffles

■ In a skillet, brown the beef, breaking up large chunks. Stir in the onion, pepper, garlic, and brown sugar. Cook until veggies are soft.

■ Mix vinegar and Worcestershire sauce together then add to skillet. Reduce heat to low and simmer for 15 minutes.

■ Add tomato paste and sauce, stirring thoroughly. Simmer for 1 hour and 30 minutes or transfer to a slow cooker and keep on low setting until ready to serve.

■ Crumble the Ruffles and sprinkle over the meat then top with bun.

sweet 'n' spicy angel-bait salsa

Think your winged guy wants Angel food cake? Think again! Take him to new heights by giving him the sweetness he craves with just a hint of naughty spice.

1 avocado, peeled and chopped

1 jalapeño pepper, minced

1 tomato, chopped

2 tbsp olive oil—extra virgin (of course)

2 tbsp lime juice

1 tsp sugar

1 mango, papaya or other fruit, diced

Shredded Manna from heaven (or, substitute coconut shavings)

■ Mix together the first six ingredients. Add the diced fruit. There are no rules here (but don't tell your Angel that—he might get twitchy). If you choose berries instead of a whole fruit, use one cup, and avoid things that brown like banana or apples. Keep refrigerated.

■ Serve over fish, steak, chicken, or even browned tortillas. Just before serving, sprinkle with Manna.

cherries à la dracones

When it comes to flambéing, no one is handier to have around than a Dragon. This delicious dessert offers you the opportunity of putting that fire breather to work. Believe me, he'll love showing off his unique skill, and the activity will work up his appetite, too.

1 pound can of pitted red cherries

¼ tsp of lemon zest

¼ tsp of orange zest

¼ tsp virgin kiss extract (if you can't find this ultra sweet ingredient, substitute vanilla)

¼ cup sugar (for cherries)

2 tbsp sugar (for cognac)

⅛ tsp cinnamon

1 tbsp arrowroot (or substitute cornstarch)

¼ cup cognac

Ice cream of choice (kept well away from his hot breath until the dish is ready to serve)

■ Drain the cherries, conserving the juice. Steep with the zests, virgin kiss (or vanilla), sugar, and cinnamon for about an hour.

■ In a stainless-steel skillet (no need for an expensive flambé pan) blend the arrowroot (or cornstarch) and 2 tbsp of cherry juice. Stir over low to medium heat, adding more cherry juice until it thickens and is warm all the way through.

■ In a separate pan, warm the cognac. Top the fruit with the warmed cognac and 2 tbsp of sugar, then give a whistle and let your Dragon do his thing. Stir until flame dies out. Serve the dish over ice cream.

■ Dragon called away? You can still enjoy this simple dessert; just fire it up with a long fireplace match. Your man might be fire retardant, but you're not.

chocolate fondue-me

If there's one thing Vampires miss, it's dessert. Thrill him to his soul (if he still has one) by turning yourself into his personal cocoa bean buffet. We promise you'll both be glad you did!

16 ounces dark, sweet, or semi-sweet chocolate

1½ cups whipping cream

1 tsp vanilla extract

Pinch of Spice of Life (should be next to sugar on the shelf of any paranormal market)

◼ Break chocolate into pieces, then combine with cream in a saucepan on medium to high heat, stirring constantly for about 3 minutes. Add vanilla and Spice of Life, continue to stir for another 3 minutes. So easy, even any immortal can do it!

◼ Your sexy Vamp can dip anything in this delicious chocolate—marshmallows, strawberries, his finger—and feed you. In turn, you can feed him from your sweetened veins. ❖

Killer Cocktails

Potent potables to slay your Dragon, slake your Vampire, or singe your Angel

The Dragon Flame

Whether you're throwing your first cocktail party with your immortal sweetie or just looking for a beverage the two of you can share on a special night, we've got some ideas for you, no matter what type of creature you're dating! Just make sure your guy is over the age of eternal consent: 300.

The Dragon Flame

This potently delicious potable possesses all the heat its name promises. Though you might find it hard to swallow, your Dragon won't be able to get enough of this one. (We recommend a milder version for humans.)

5 oz gin
1 oz vermouth
30 drops Tabasco sauce (for Dragons)
15 drops Tabasco sauce (for humans)
Splash of Everclear Dragon Potion (or substitute any white rum)
Some Dragon firebreath or a match for the flambé

Mix the gin and vermouth in an iced shaker with the Tabasco. Pour into a large martini glass before adding the floater of Everclear or rum, then step back and have your guy breathe a little fire over the top to light it up. Drink as soon as the fire subsides for a warm and pleasurable burn down your throat.

The Angeltini

This classic is perfect for those heavenly immortals who have spent most of their lives in the clouds. Not only will the blue sky color of the drink with its coconut shaving "cloud" remind them of home, but the sweetness will delight their good-boy senses.

2 oz Bombay Sapphire gin
1 oz blue curaçao liqueur
6 ice cubes
Powdered sugar to rim the glass
1 tbsp fresh coconut, shaved

Pour the gin and curaçao into a cocktail shaker filled with ice and shake well. Wet the rim of the martini glass and rim with powdered sugar. Then strain the liquid into the glass and finish by dropping the shaved coconut on top for garnish.

The Dirty Devil

We think this is the drink for modern Demons who can go all night long and drink anyone under the table. To satisfy their diabolical urges, they need something hellishly hot, yet with enough sweetness to keep their darkest drives in check. Everyone knows that a Demon can't resist temptation…but you won't be able to, either, after one or two of these.

1 shot of vodka
1 shot of jalapeño tequila
1 shot of Jägermeister
1 shot of Demon Wrath (substitute fruit punch for you)
1 tsp equal parts ground cayenne pepper and sugar, mixed

Put all of the ingredients except the pepper/sugar mixture into a chilled shaker and shake thoroughly. Wet the rims of martini glasses and rim with the mix of cayenne pepper and sugar, then fill and drink up!

The Zone Out

This one is our favorite pick for Zombies and the humans who love them. The potent blend of flavors and textures might knock you flat on your back—but you'll get up with a smile (and maybe a good story for next month's Strange But True column).

- **1 cup fresh blood (or substitute red wine)**
- **1 oz wormwood absinthe**
- **½ cup diced figs, dates, and blood orange sections**

Put all of the ingredients into a blender and blend on a low speed for ten seconds. (If you aren't as fond of pulp as your Zombie surely is, blend a little bit longer.) Pour into a highball glass.

Bloodiest Mary Ever

This Vamp-pleaser is a tasty substitute for you (if that's the way you want to play it) *and* great for get-togethers with his crowd. We guarantee it will have your be-fanged boyfriend wishing he were human again!

- **2 oz vodka**
- **4 oz blood (substitute tomato juice for the mortals in the crowd)**
- **Juice from half a lemon**
- **½ tsp prepared horseradish**
- **Dash of Worcestershire sauce**
- **Dash of Tabasco sauce**
- **1 pinch each of salt, pepper and celery salt**
- **Celery stalk and lime wedge for garnish**

Combine all ingredients except garnish in a cocktail shaker with ice. Shake vigorously. Strain over ice cubes in a tall glass. Garnish with a celery stalk and a lime wedge and have extra pepper and blood for those who crave a little more of a tang.

Wolfbane Lager

This isn't a recipe—just a suggestion. Wolfbane is a potent yet smooth beer with just the right amount of alcohol and toxin to get your Were riled in all the right ways. If you are dating a wolf, don't get caught without at least a six-pack for that unexpected midnight drop-in. In fact—get a case, as he's likely to bring a pack of friends. (Remember what happened when the beer ran low last time, and they started fighting over the last can? You do NOT want your neighbors to call the cops again.) ❖

Gifted Ghouls Give GoDieVa

Tempting, tasty, and oh-so sweet…that's you, to your out-of-this world lover. You may be his favorite treat, but we know yours: GoDieVa Chocolates. From our luscious Dark-and-Stormy Truffles to our heavenly Angel Flake Bon-Bons and sinfully spicy Cinnamon Kisses, we have the devilish delights you crave—and your beastly beau loves to give. Nothing makes an LG's mouth water like a classic silver box of GoDieVa.

GoDieVa Chocolates . . . diabolically delicious!

Once Bitten

A True Story of Paranormal Romance

Tiffany Bainbridge

Every month, we are happy to bring you a true story from one of our readers about her experiences in the romantic underworld. This month's delicious offering comes from a loyal and lovely reader from Ames, Iowa. Keep pursuing your dream guys—and keep sending us your stories!

I never wanted to be *that* girl. The one people shake their heads at in public, the one other women make catty remarks about, the one who looks gloriously, ridiculously happy . . . because the man she's with is just a little bit more than the average guy. He's immortal.

We've all thought about it, if we're honest. What it might be like to walk hand in hand in the moonlight with a guy whose life is more storybook fantasy than nine-to-five reality. A guy who really is faster than a speeding bullet, stronger than a Hollywood action hero, and always on the sexy side of dangerous.

My immortal turned out to be a Vampire. We met at my job. I'm a florist, and he's got a thing for roses. Every Friday night, week after week, he'd stop by, always the last customer of the day as the

store was closing for the night, and pick up a dozen or two. At first, I thought he was a player out to impress all his different dates. What else would a guy that hot be doing with all those roses?

When I finally got up the courage to ask him what he did with all those flowers, he told me they were for his home. That he loved the smell of roses, the beauty of them, and that having fresh flowers reminded him of the daylight world he hadn't seen in over five hundred years.

We met at my job. I'm a florist, and he's got a thing for roses.

My heart did that beat-skipping thing. He was so sincere, I couldn't doubt him. Which meant I had been completely wrong about him. So, the next Friday, to make up for all the bad thoughts I'd had, I pulled the most beautiful roses from our daily shipment and set them aside for him. (What he normally got at the end of the day wasn't our best stock.) When he came in that night, I surprised him with them. He showed his appreciation by asking me out.

I hesitated. Why me? Would he try to bite me? What would people think? What did you wear to date a Vampire? In the end, I said yes, as much out of curiosity as attraction.

We went to dinner, where I was not the main course. The restaurant was intimate and expensive, and they treated us like rock stars. After dinner, we strolled the city streets, window shopping and talking about our lives. He is not only the best-dressed man I've ever seen, he is also the most interesting man I've ever met. I could listen to the stories of his life for hours, but he kept saying he'd rather hear about my life and my dreams. Again I wondered why. I'm so . . . boring. So average.

Still, we kept dating and I kept falling deeper, forgetting all my past prejudices and not caring that other humans called me his "sippy cup." He was amazing, always surprising me with little presents (like a diamond bangle bracelet from DeKay Jewelers and a pair of Jimmy Chew boots I'd been coveting) for no reason other than he thought I would like them. And yes, I got a lot of roses, too. He was a little old fashioned in some ways—always opened doors, stood when I entered the room, pulled out my chair—and it was charming to be attended to that way, I have to tell you. I felt special. Like more than just his date, but somehow, the center of his world. Crazy? Maybe, but that's how he made me feel.

Things progressed and little milestones came and went. Our first kiss (wow), our first night together (amazing!), the first time he bit me (un-freaking-

believable). The whole blood thing, which I thought would creep me out, was suddenly no big deal. I became more of a night owl, and he got a spray tan.

Six months into the relationship, he asked me to marry him. That was two years ago and I'm still madly in love. That kind of giddy, stars-seem-brighter, glowy kind of love. I don't care that he's a Vampire. All that matters is how sweet and wonderful he is, how taking care of me always seems like his first priority.

Things progressed and little milestones came and went. Our first kiss (wow), our first night together (amazing!), the first time he bit me (un-freaking-believable).

I don't know what the future holds yet, but I know that my days in the sun are numbered. He's going to live forever and I'm . . . not. Unless . . . . When I'm ready, I just might take him up on his long-standing offer to turn me into a Vampire. How could I not? Eternity with one man is a very long time, yes, but he's so much more than just a man. He's everything I've ever wanted in a guy.

Am I scared? A little. But let's face it, I've already become that girl. Being her for the rest of time wouldn't be such a bad thing after all. Plus I have him to guide me.

One final thing. He bought the flower shop I used to work in and gave it to me as a wedding gift. I now own and operate the only all-night florist in town. We changed the name to Late Bloomers. Fitting, don't you think? ❖

Dragon Gold and Angel Dust

How to Get and Keep Your Own Eternal Cha-Ching

Stephania Franco created the first pre-immortal-focused investment firm after meeting and marrying her Vampire husband, Luciano. Currently she manages the $2.7 billion ForeverMutual Pre-Immortal Life or Death Fund. We asked her the best way an LG can make sure her cash stash grows to eternal proportions before taking the big afterlife plunge because, after all, how much dough is really enough when you're planning to live forever (and you don't necessarily want to rely on your Changer for your pocket change)? Here's what she had to say.

Anyone who tells you money can't buy happiness is lying. It can. It can also buy you food, clothes, and shelter—things that are far more important in death than they ever were in life. You don't want the sun to blister your soon-to-be-super-sensitive skin, do you?

A smart, savvy LG knows she must sit down and ask her forever-after man how he supports his own stylish afterlife. Does your Dragon have a dungeon full of pirate gold? Is your Angel hoarding some of Michelangelo's unknown works? Did your Zombie help Steve Jobs work out some of Apple's kinks—for a piece of the action? Does your Werewolf have shares of any stock traded exclusively on the OSM (Otherworld Stock Market)?

If his answer is yes, you've got one more question for him: Will he help you with your nest egg? (Just don't use that terminology with a Dragon or the only reply you're likely to get is *goodbye*.) Chances are good that your man has plenty to spare. And if he's willing to share his heart with you, why not his treasure, too?

"But Stephania," I hear some of you say. "I want to be responsible for my *own* finances, not rely on some night-stalking sugar daddy to take care of me." Well, all right, then. First order of business is finding a money manager or broker you trust. And I mean trust enough to tell him the real reason for your money concern. You won't be able to trade on

the OSM until you're actually immortal, but there are other things you can do, and a savvy investment expert who is hip to the underworld (or possibly even undead himself) can definitely help.

One of the first things your advisor will tell you is that you should be saving. In my mind, fifteen percent of your paycheck is a great number to shoot for. Put five percent into a simple savings account for emergencies, unexpected bills arising from fire or rampage damage to your condo, etc., and put ten percent into some kind of mutual fund with moderate risk and decent growth potential. You never know how long you're going to live and you can withdraw this centuries after death, all the while watching it increase over the eons of time.

That's the "safety" part of your money plan, but try to scrape together a few thousand dollars each year to invest in a riskier arena: stocks and bonds. (No, I'm not talking about bondage, you silly Demon-lover.) If you don't trust your knowledge of the mortal markets, rely on that broker to help you select the right portfolio. Here's a tip: invest in businesses you trust personally. Because I'm married to a Vamp, my portfolio is full of companies that provide medical services—blood banks, organ banks, medical supplies, etc. My Dragon friend recently bought stock in a company that makes flame-retardant garments for firefighters, and my Zombie-obsessed colleague can't say enough about her stock in Frito-Lay and Olive Garden. Get the picture?

There's one last thing to think about: Protection. Just because your man has promised to make you immortal and be by your side forever doesn't mean your relationship will be

without problems. Take care of yourself and iron out any potential legal issues *before* the big change. (Mortals call it a pre-nup; the undead call it a pre-mort.)

Here's an example of why you should get your mind off hearts and stakes for a few minutes and get some guidelines down on parchment. A few years ago, a married couple I know paid a Vampire to turn them both. (Yep, some immortals make a killing that way.) Fast-forward another few years and the once-human couple is in the middle of a nasty divorce. The husband claims their transformations have rendered them both legally dead and he shouldn't have to pay alimony.

What you should know: According to the American Vampire Council, that is absolutely not the case. If something like this happens to you, be sure to cite Martin *vs.* Martin, in which the wife was turned and the husband, who was not, tried to stop paying alimony the moment she was declared legally dead. In that landmark case, the judge decreed that when one or both spouses become immortal, economical responsibility continues regardless of either bodies' physical state. But the whole dilemma (and all of those legal fees) could have been avoided with a well-rendered pre-mort mapping out what happens in the unlikely event of a post-change split. Just as there are financial advisors with an expertise in undead issues, there are immortalist lawyers as well. Don't be afraid to contact an AVC-approved attorney, let him know you're soon to be turned, and have him draft a contract you both feel comfortable with. If your creature balks at this . . . think hard about taking the big plunge. You don't want an eternity of legal and financial troubles. ❖

after *Lifetime*

From brand-new programming to classic television, to your favorite

drop
dead
devil

how i
bit your
mother

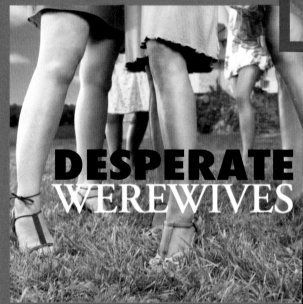

DESPERATE
WEREWIVES

Network

The Shows You Crave When He's Out on the Prowl

movies and specials, we've got a lineup fit for a queen of the night!

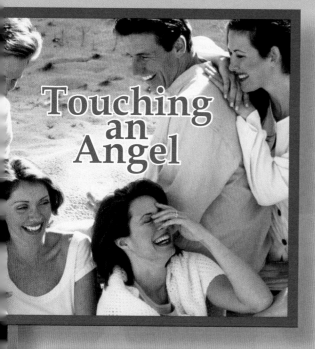

Touching an Angel

the **Real Vampires** OF VEGAS

the old adventures of **undeadchristine**

Off the Set with

the Real Vampires OF VEGAS

Your favorite TV Vamps let their hair down about the
late-night parties, the fang fights, the fashion—
and all those irresistible, immortal men.

Everyone loves the new hit series *The Real Vampires of Vegas*! The beauty, the decadence, the drama . . . and we're assured that every moment of it is genuine, spontaneous, and unscripted. (We so want to believe that, don't we?)

The show's immortal stars, plucked from obscurity to live out their crazy lives on the screen, have captivated millions of fans and taken reality TV to a whole new level of hell. We can't stop obsessing over these Vamp Tramps (as they call themselves) and their fluctuating friendships, boy toy wars, millennia-old grudges, and unbelievable riches. Oh, the riches! These be-fanged beauties really know how to live—as it were.

We went behind the scenes and off camera to get you the juicy gossip and secret hijinks they can't show you on TV. So—read on for the real scoop on the Farrow vs. Nadesda fang fight, what goes on behind closed doors with Goria and her string of immortal flings, and much more. We're dedicated to bringing you the whole scoop on those Vampires we love to hate but would love to be!

Farrow vs. Nadesda— What You Didn't See on TV

We all saw the now infamous incident when Nadesda "accidentally" spilled blood on Farrow's Cleopatra chair—an actual gift from the Egyptian queen. In a crazy blur of *superinhuman* speed and strength, Farrow tackled Nadesda and the spandex started to fly, reminding us that these ladies have awesome power hiding under that flawless pale skin. (No spray tans on *this* reality show!)

The fang fight that ensued was one of the highlights of the season, a screeching tornado of destruction that utterly obliterated Farrow's ultra-enviable penthouse apartment at the pulsing heart of the Vegas strip. But what the cameras DIDN'T catch was even more amazing.

According to Farrow, earlier that night she and Nadesda had been stalking the casinos for some handsome and willing donors to party with. Nadesda found a few boys in town from the Big Apple and "being the greedy, jealous Vampling she is, she wanted the humans all to herself." So she snuck off camera with her fresh prey, leaving Farrow hungry and solo.

"Nadesda is so easy to track, it's a joke," Farrow snickered when telling her side of the story to our on-set insider. "She leaves a blood and underwear trail like she's Gretel. And you should have seen her face when I burst into the hotel room just a few minutes behind her and the boys. She tried to play it cool, but she was obviously furious. I, of course, had my pick of the litter and left

Nads with the boring-as-hell banker who you just know tasted like Big Macs."

They made up, though—or so Farrow thought. They took some blood to go, heading back to her place to beat the sunrise. That's where the cameras caught up with them—just in time to see Nadesda slosh some of her leftovers onto Farrow's favorite royal antique. Nadesda maintains that it was a simple accident. She was a little tipsy from the alcohol infused blood they had just downed and got a little sloppy. She claims she has no idea what "sweet, deluded Fare" is talking about. She barely even remembers the city slickers they were sampling, except for the fact that their tastes ran to Bludweiser more than Veuve type-O champagne.

Was it a blood vendetta?

A simple accident? All we know for sure is that it made for some good entertainment!

Goria and the Gorgeous Georges

It's no secret that Goria is considered the "pretty one" on the show, much to the dismay of the rest of the cast. They're all super-beauties, of course, but Goria seems to have captivated the mortal and immortal public alike with her ethereal blond beauty, smashing vintage wardrobe, and flawless complexion. She may look as if she spends all of her waking hours primping, but don't be fooled—Goria manages to find time to get up to some pretty crazy tricks. A tigress through and through, she is the perfect predator of love. You've seen it yourself, week after week. Men—living and

undead—throw themselves at her perfectly pedicured feet while she stays cool, collects them at her whim, and discards them when they are too pale and exhausted to amuse her further.

But what does Goria actually *do* with all her suitors? We asked this man-eater ourselves to find out.

DTU: So, Goria, you attract a million men a minute and they all want to bare their souls (and necks) to you. How do you find time for all the gorgeous guys that catch your eye?

Goria: [chuckles] It's not *that* many men. The show really edits my life to make it look like an endless parade, but I definitely keep some "me" time in my schedule. I admit, my calendar is pretty full, but I try to keep Sunday and Monday nights for myself and the girls. Tuesday through Thursday I go on at least two dates per night. The first one is usually someone I'm casually interested in. If there's a middleman, he's usually lowest on my list—just a source of nourishment or a "snack,"

as I like to think of it. And the guy I end my night with, well, he's my real pick for the evening. Friday and Saturday nights I always keep open, so I can go where the party takes me. I recommend this schedule to any girl, Vamp or LG, who likes to keep her options open!

DTU: Wow, that's a lot of dates! What do you generally do when you go out with a guy?

Goria: That depends on the guy. If he's rich, we go shopping. I model what I want or what he picks out for me, and he usually ends up buying it (and carrying it, of course). If he's a Vampire, we might do a little hunting together, just for the exercise. But Vampires can be so boring. First of all, they always want to tell stuffy old stories about famous historical people they knew. Who cares!? I knew Genghis too, and the guy was a total pig. Secondly, most of us have been around for so long that it gets a little incestuous—everyone's dated everyone and it can get messy. My favorite dates are with guys

that are sweet as sugar, hot as hell, and dumb as rocks. (Do I have to tell you that most of them are mortal?) We don't have to make small talk, we just have fun dancing and dining.

DTU: Okay, we get it. You are living the life. But you must want to settle down at some point and curl up in the coffin with Mr. Right for all eternity. Have you ever had a serious boyfriend? Do you find yourself wanting one now?

Goria: Oh, of course I've had some serious relationships in my time. You can't be around for thousands of years without falling hard once or twice. I was with the same guy from 1678–1843. Then I got stuck in a rebound relationship with the wrong guy, a real player, and the next thing I knew, it was the 1960s! I learned that no matter how interesting and wild a guy is, after a century or two, I start to get the itch. Think about it—who really wants to sleep with the same guy for eternity? That's forever, people! I prefer to imagine life as an all-you-can-eat

buffet. But ask me again in a few hundred years—maybe I'll have slowed down by then.

Mariasha's Battle with Bloodorexia

Last week everyone was talking as much about what wasn't on the show as what was. We're referring, of course, to Mariasha's unexplained absence. We tried to get in touch with her but her agent is being very secretive and will only say that she is "in need of a little rest and a little privacy."

But Mariasha's battle with bloodorexia is no secret. Her fellow Real Vampires have talked about it pretty openly on camera, whenever she was out of earshot. A healthy Vampire should feed every night to keep her strength up, but according to her castmates' reports, Mariasha would feed only once or twice a week and then only in carefully measured spoonfuls of blood from athletes or vegetarians.

"We're all in excellent shape, that's part of being a Vampire, but Mariasha seems

to think perfect isn't good enough," said Farrow when questioned about Mariasha's disorder. "We try to talk to her about it, but she just flies into a rage and denies it. It's so sad."

An unnamed source close to this tragic story blamed Mariasha's absence from the show on the loss of a tooth—a sign of an escalating problem. According to the report, the tooth lost wasn't a fang but a canine, so it won't require major surgery—but anyone familiar with the symptoms of bloodorexia knows that the teeth are the first thing to go in situations of severe Vampire malnourishment. Apparently, Mariasha is resting at a clinic where she has been sedated and is being fed intravenously.

The producers of *Real Vampires* and the network have made no comment as to how long she might be absent from the festivities, but previews for next week's episode introduce a new Vampire—Cherry—a flame-haired supermodel fresh in town from Prague. Rumors are flying that she will be Mariasha's replacement.

Kayla's Late Nights and Close Calls

The Real Vampires' resident party girl is Kayla all the way. She knows all the hottest clubs, has been spotted with such celebrities as Orlando Bloom and Hayden Christiansen, and was recently photographed in the VIP section of a rooftop bar getting close to another on-camera Vamp, Robert Pattinson. (We hear he's made the transition to real Vamp, and we couldn't be happier!)

But is Kayla spinning out of control? Last week's *Creeple Magazine* showed her running down a dawn-streaked street holding a newspaper overhead to block the sun's rays. Goria had this to say: "I say let her have her fun. I mean, do you know how long it takes for sunburn to fade on a Vampire? Years! In fact, the only thing that can age our skin is the sun. At this rate, she'll get crow's feet, and who would want to date a wrinkly Vamp when the rest of us are flawless!? That means more for me."

We caught up with Kayla just as she was getting into her custom fuchsia limo, and she was kind enough to offer us a ride and a few minutes of conversation. We couldn't wait to ask her about the rumors of party overkill.

"LGs and MMs love to watch the people, they wish they could be going to the parties, they wish they could get into and talk to the people they wish they could get close to. Most people are wishers, but I'm one of the lucky few living the afterlife!" At that point she giggled, then paused to take a few sips from her giant cup of Plazbuck's.

"And that makes them jealous. They love to see someone like me take a spill. Just look at how the papers are treating poor Mariasha. They'll cling to any story they hear and blow it so way out of proportion, or take any overheard conversation or sex tape totally out of context. When it comes to me, reality is far better than any fiction. That's why they put me on TV. But the way they spin it—that I'm losing control, taking it too far—honey, I can't take it too far, I'm an immortal! So . . . ? I stayed out past curfew by accident one night. *Everyone* loses track of time at the tables in the casinos. Seriously, people need to get a grip."

At that point, the limo (Kayla calls it her "batmobile") pulled up to Vx2—the most exclusive club in all of Vegas. It was only 1:00 in the morning, but already the lines wrapped around the block. Black leather-clad attendants clambered to open the door and escort Kayla past the Dragon bouncers and hordes of screaming fans. She didn't even glance in their direction—just tossed her paper cup, imprinted with her bright red lip prints, into the crowd.

We don't know about you, but we can't wait for next season to find out what's new in their world! ❖

Undead and Well-Read

What's Hot Between the Covers This Month

by Juno Jones

Are you ready for a whole new crop of entrancing fiction all about your favorite undead heroes? We've been burning the midnight oil reading every new novel out there, and these are our picks for the beach, the bus, or under the covers with a flashlight while he's on a midnight romp.

Revenge of the Sexy, Scary (SEXY) Fire Dragon
by Ava Donnelly

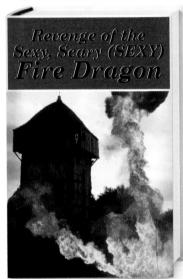

King of the Fire Dragons, Dante Wyvern, is in a bad mood—and the only thing that seems to help is burning picturesque villages to the ground, then retiring to his cave to watch *You've Got Mail* on DVD. That is, until he meets Catherine Holloway, whose vulnerable beauty lights his flame in a new (and somewhat less dangerous) way. After about five minutes of small talk and an epic romp that levels a local rainforest, she promises to love him forever. But when she weds his arch enemy the very next day . . . well . . . let's just say that things heat up again for those poor villagers. Revenge burns hot and fast in this searing sequel to *My Kingdom for a Sexy, Scary (SEXY) Fire Dragon*. Grab your oven mitts before turning to page 1!

Eat, Pray, Slay
by Michelle Quine

Modern day Demon-hunter Margarette Dawson knows a little something about a good slay. Ever since a horde of Demons disappeared with her twin sister, she's been on a rampage for blood. Yeah, yeah, she got the memo that not all Demons are evil, and it's time to flush her holy water, but she's not buying. That is, until gorgeous Xavier Santanos struts through the door. He's one hundred percent Demon sex appeal and claims to know where her sister is imprisoned. He says he's willing to help her . . . for a wicked night in her bed. Will Margarette find heaven in Xavier's arms? Passion and intrigue combine to create a sizzling love-hate tug-of-war as two unlikely allies finally give in to temptation.

The Virgin's Secret Werewolf Babies
by Karen Loman

Emily Thompson is a librarian by day—and a stripper by night. Ever since her selfish sister signed over custody of her Werewolf nephews, she's had to bump and grind to pay for diapers. This spunky bookworm daydreams of a happy ending for her new family, until the boys' father bursts on the scene, determined to possess Emily by fair means or foul, and she realizes those dreams have been clawed to shreds. How can the Alpha of the Lunar Mist pack love a woman he clearly doesn't respect? And what happens when her sister tries to reclaim her kids just so *she* can marry the Alpha? Don't miss this ravishing tale of heartbreak, sibling rivalry, and redemption.

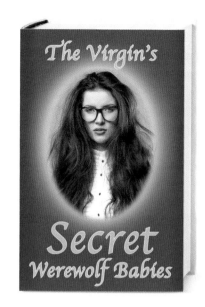

Heaven's Fury
by Jennifer Seitsinger

When Lillian Merryweather witnesses a Demonic ritual, the clumsy barista becomes a target for elimination and is quickly assigned a bodyguard—a sexy guardian Angel named Christophe tasked with getting her to the heavenly hearing in seven days. Preferably alive. Chased through jungles, erotic nightclubs, and even her ex's backyard— WTF?—the two battle Demon assassins as they try to hold off their own wicked desires. Watching a good boy turn bad will keep you flipping the pages of this madcap thriller that ends with (spoiler alert!) the perfect shiver of forbidden romance.

Her Dark Seducer's Eternal Kiss
by Shonna Hurt

Known as the Devil's Evil Twin, Vladimir is the only Vampire in existence to remain hideously scarred after his transformation. Now every meal is a lesson in humiliation. He approaches, and women run. Needless to say, constant hunger has made him . . . cranky. In desperation, he turns to Veins for Hire and Sophia Smith becomes his weekly meal-on-wheels. From day one he is captivated by her grace, wit, and charm— but how can a beast like him ever win such a beauty's heart? Soul-meltingly romantic, this beauty-and-the-beast will leave you panting for more—and wishing your own Vampire had a few imperfections to keep your blood sizzling throughout eternity. ❖

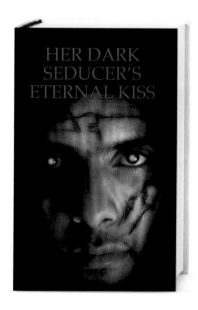

Zombitos

Don't Call It
"Junk Food!"

*'Fess up—you love **Zombitos** as much as he does! The tang, the crunch, the salty orange goodness . . . go ahead, eat them by the bagful. Eat them for breakfast. (We won't tell.)*

Now in four Zombie-lovin' flavors:
Original, Barbecue, Carrion, and Brain Matter!

13 Places to Go Before You Don't Die

Must-See Destinations and Adventures of a Lifetime for You and Your Immortal Sweetheart

Your undead honey may have all the time in the world, but you don't (at least not until you take that final plunge). You live on the edge and you love a little bit of danger once in awhile. That's why it is high time for you to come up with a travel "bucket list"—an itinerary of must-sees before taking that eternal dirt nap. It may sound a little morbid, but let's face it, we're into that, too.

Bucket lists are great because they allow you to focus on your big dreams right now, rather than relegating them to some "rainy day" in the future. Let your mind wander to those lavish vacations and once-in-a-lifetime adventures you've drooled over—and start making a list. Once you're keeping track of the things you are (avoiding) dying to do, you're more likely to *do* them! Plus, you'll realize how much is waiting for you out there—and how little time you have to experience it all. (At least in *this* lifetime.) You'll stop daydreaming and get going!

We've compiled our own list to help you get started, but you are bound to come up with many more great ideas. And since you are an LG with a taste for the undead, we've tailored our picks to include things you can do with your favorite immortal. Our choices are exciting, beautiful, and have a supernatural flair—just like your post-mortem paramour, heavenly-bodied boy, or world-wizened wolf. You'll be asking your boss for vacation time and packing your bags before you've even finished reading it, guaranteed.

1 Trek through the Yukon to Check Out the Aurora Borealis

Every spring and fall equinox the Yukon hosts an amazing lightshow whose beauty is unrivaled in the natural world. Colors dance across an ever-morphing sky of perpetual darkness. Passion-fruit pink, emerald green, breathtaking cerulean—colors that would shame a rainbow burn the sky, making for an unforgettable sight. And the best part? Your Vamp sweetheart can watch this awe-inspiring display right along with you—unlike those sunsets and sunrises he always has to miss. Not to get all technical, but the Aurora Borealis (or Northern Lights) are made up of particles thrown out by the sun, sucked into the earth's magnetic field, and pulled to the north pole, only to collide with our atmosphere and erupt in a dazzling display. The short version is—it's *light* but it isn't *sunlight*. He'll be eternally grateful to you for sharing the experience with him—and he can fly you there in no time, minus the baggage charge and stale peanuts!

2 Race Across Alaska in Your Own Iditarod

They say a canine that gets a lot of exercise is a well-behaved companion. The same is true for your Werewolf boyfriend. The more he gets to stretch his legs, the happier he will be. So yoke your honey and a few of his friends to a sled, pile on the coats, and check out the beautiful state of Alaska. The landscapes are incredible—glowing glaciers, majestic mountains, vast prairies, glass-topped lakes. Picturesque is an understatement when it comes to describing the wonders that await you to the north. And with your muscular mate towing you along, you can relax and enjoy the view! (Plus, he's just the guy to keep you warm and toasty at night.) Just make sure to pack plenty of fresh meat and energy bars so he doesn't fade before you make camp each night.

3 Scuba Dive through the Ruins of Atlantis

Yes, it exists! The enchanting city of Atlantis may have been lost to us humans for a couple millennia, but it's remained a favorite top-secret destination for immortals. Go ahead—ask your boyfriend. He may be reluctant to disclose the location, but if you ask very sweetly (while wearing that killer mini-dress that makes his mouth water), your sweetheart might just whisk you away to this slice of paradise. Picture a place with the style of the Parthenon, the artistry of Byzantium, and the decadence of ancient Rome—then multiply that by a thousand, and you'll start to get a sense of the place: a glorious sunken city surrounded by turquoise water alive with otherworldly creatures and coral rainbows. As you explore the underwater glories of this lost world, you'll finally feel what it's like to fly. Just one no-no: Leave the camera at home!

4. Skinny Dip in the Hot Springs of the Arenal Volcano in Costa Rica

This trip will carry you near the equator—making it a perfect way to heat things up with your Dragon or Demon dreamboat. The jungles of Costa Rica are home to the active Arenal Volcano, a bubbling beast that offers dozens of natural hot tubs for you and your hot-blooded honey to unwind in. (Pack the asbestos bathing suit, just in case.) You'll be relaxing in mother nature's own spa—and if tempers flare or things go metaphorically south with your red-hot lover, you're sure to encounter a few Angels in the nearby cloud forest, ready to catch you on the rebound.

5. Plant a Tree in the Garden of Eden

Again . . . yes, it exists—if you have an Angel to guide you there, that is. This virgin forest is so beautiful, you are bound to weep—so bring a box of tissues or you'll have to use his wings to dry your cheeks. The enchanting trees seem to stretch endlessly up into the heavens, every flower is always in perfect bloom, and the animals are downy soft and waiting to nuzzle you. And if you've been working on getting your Angel to doff his halo and let his guard down a little in the bedroom, here's an idea: Find the nearest apple tree and pluck the reddest, juiciest fruit you can find. He won't be able to resist it—or you—for a second. Here's another plus—no packing because no clothing! You'll be feasting your eyes on each other *au naturel*, bathed in the spiritually infused sunlight that radiates throughout this magical place. Dare we say it? It's heaven on earth.

6. Scout out Loch Ness and Search for Your Dragon's Reclusive Friend

The Scottish Highlands comprise one of the most underrated sites in the world. The emerald green hills, rocky cliffs, pristine lakes, and antique castles make for a truly magical vacation, especially if you have a Dragon in tow. You'll feel transported to a different era; a time when maidens were really maidens and Dragons ruled the skies. Your beastie boy will feel so at home here that he may even take you to meet that infamous recluse, Nessy. Warning! Nessy does NOT like to be called the Loch Ness Monster, the Monster of Loch Ness, or anything involving the M word. That's half the reason she (yes, she!) went into hiding in the first place.

7. Take a Haunted Tour of New Orleans

NoLa is a charming city full of elegant architecture, incredible history, and some deep dark secrets that your Vampire knows all about. Home to one of the first American Vampire communities and the epicenter of voodoo in the U.S., New Orleans is rich in his history as well as yours. You can visit the centuries-old cemeteries and crypts and stay at one of the many "haunted" hotels. (They almost always have wickedly good restaurants where you can enjoy the best food and spirits while on the lookout for . . . spirits.) Your Vamp will be stoked to show you around—and if you're currently sans-Vamp, you'll have no trouble meeting one down there. This is a good destination to share with a Zombie, as well—you can enjoy the sights while he makes an appointment with one of the many voodoo priestesses who specialize in limb re-inforcement. Even Dragons and Demons enjoy New Orleans for its hot, steamy summers, and the swamps are a real draw for Weres. Whatever your taste, your jaunt down to the Big Easy is sure to make it easier to get a little bit closer to your immortal hottie.

8. Explore the Catacombs of Paris

Prefer an undead trip abroad? Then nothing tops the City of Lights. This twinkling European gem, famed for its romantic and artistic history, is home to such marvels as the Arc de Triomphe, the Louvre, and the infamous Parisian catacombs. This awesome ossuary is a winding network of stone- and bone-lined passages that weave a spider web through the Paris underground. Regular walking tours are available, but your undead paramour probably has some first-hand knowledge of the place—he may even recognize some of the permanent residents that decorate the passageways. So let him show off his expertise of this wonder, and keep your ears open for some of the details of his personal history you've always wondered about.

9. Tour the Doritos Factory in Killingly, Connecticut

If you've fallen head over heels for a Zombie, you probably have some similar interests, including video games, lots of TV, and that crunchy, cheesy, tasty miracle food known as Doritos. You also probably have a tough time finding a good reason to get off the couch, but trust me, you absolutely have to take a pilgrimage to the mecca of snack foods, the Doritos factory. On your own guided tour, you will witness the birth of these delicious chips, sample new experimental flavors, and taste the freshest Doritos on the planet—still warm off the factory line!

10 Battle the Tomb Warriors of China

A trip to the Far East and immersion in a foreign culture is just the trick to shake up your world view and expand your horizons, especially in the company of someone who has been around as long as the famed Terracotta Army of Xi'an. This massive regiment of over 8,000 soldiers was created by Emperor Qín Ling, more than two hundred years before Christ, to protect him in the afterlife. Who knows? Your dude might have helped design them! If you are an LG with a taste for archaeology, you'll have a great time taking in this extraordinary monument created by a culture obsessed with undeath!

11 Adventure across Tanzania on a Wild Safari

It's called the Dark Continent—so how can it be bad? For the truly adventurous LG, the land that is home to the magical plains of the Serengeti, the fury of Mount Kilimanjaro, and the natural secluded beauty of Zanzibar is absolutely a must-see. You can take a Serengeti safari—a hunting trip any Were-guy would die for—and get an up-close-and-personal view of some awesome animal behavior (and maybe some ideas for the bedroll). Or, if you like the view from on high, take a trek up Mount Kili, on foot or on your Werewolf's back. Any Dragon worth his fire would be thrilled to take you to the heart of the volcanic action, which is plentiful in Africa. Or if you just want to chill out with your Zombie, you can stretch out on the pristine shores of Zanzibar.

12 Relax to the Max in Shangri-La

This legendary utopia is hands down the most luxurious place on earth. The air is pure oxygen, the water is wine, and everywhere you look there's a five-star something. The catch? Its location in the Kunlun Mountains of China is a well-guarded secret that only the richest and most powerful undeads know. The worst hotel in Shangri-La makes the Four Seasons look like a Motel 6. Crude gestures like the exchange of money aren't tolerated—you are allowed in only on the credit of your good name and annual generous donations. So if you want to experience the unsurpassed elegance and opulence of this hidden paradise, you better start your hunt for the guy who can get you in!

13 Take a Hot-Air Balloon Ride Over the Castles of Transylvania

No LG with a taste for the undead could ever call herself well-traveled without a trip to Transylvania. Let's face it though, it's a little bit dreary there and sort of hard to get around. That's why the best way to see it is via hot air balloon. From your rattan aerie, you can take in the countryside, the castles, the winding roads, and everything Transylvania has to offer as you float serenely on the breeze. Your Vamp guide can point out all the best landmarks from your celestial vantage point, and your allergies won't act up from the centuries-old dust coating every surface of every ancient castle. If the two of you are apprehensive about flying unguided, skilled Dragons are available and useful, as they provide the heat that keeps the balloon aloft, replacing those noisy propane tanks. ❖

traveloddity,
Take Us Away!

Dating the undead presents unique challenges at vacation time—so LGs in the know turn to traveloddity.

- Vacationing with your Vampire? Check out Antarctica in winter, where the sun never comes up and you can cuddle for warmth 24/7.

- Your Dragon will marvel at the Castle District in Austria—just like a home away from home— right down to the luxury dungeon accommodations!

- Don't put off that delicious spa vacation with your Zombie, where you'll get pampered while he gets reattached.

- Wish you could fly alongside your Angel? Try parasailing together in the Bahamas, where you can both take wing.

New specials everyday—just click and fly!

IMMORSTROLOGY

Our Indispensable Guide to the Heavenly Bodies That Guide THEIR Heavenly Bodies—and Yours!

"Hey, baby, what's your sign?"

Unless you've never gone to a bar, a frat party, or attended high school, you've heard this cheesy pick up line. And once upon a time, you probably rolled your eyes and laughed about the answer. But, for anyone dating an immortal or simply looking to score with one, compatibility is oh, so important . . . to survival. So, whether your tastes run toward fiercely protective Werewolves or peerlessly perfect Angels (or any other irresistible breed), you need to know who's right for you—and who isn't.

You probably know your own Zodiac sign and a little something about its characteristics, but did you know that immortals each have a sign and constellation that governs their behavior as well? Here's the rundown on the celestial bodies associated with each major species of the undead, along with a little about their star-driven natures.

Phoenix—Sign of the Vampire

The Phoenix is a mythological bird that dies only to be reborn from its own ashes. Found in the southern sky, this constellation is most often associated with the Vampire. Perhaps that's why there is so much myth-information flying around (as it were) about Vampires turning into bats, etc. Vamps are incredibly resilient, often jaded (as only someone who has lived a very long life can be), but desperate to find that special lady who will make them feel young forever more.

Lupus—Sign of the Werewolf

Werewolves are ruled by the constellation Lupus, which resides in the southern sky, near Centaurus and Scorpio. The ancient Babylonians sometimes referred to it as the Mad Dog, and a Were approaching his change can appear to be just that. Werewolves feel most comfortable outside in the elements, even when they are in their human form. They desire a return to nature, and love nothing better than

naps under the shade of a large oak tree or long hikes without a map or cell phone. Fiercely loyal, once mated, it's for life.

Draco—Sign of the Dragon

Draco, the sign associated with Dragons, can be found in the northern sky. Many myths and legends surround Draco, but from one time to another, one culture to another, one story persists. Draco once guarded precious golden apples in a garden tended by the daughter of Atlas. The fearless protector Dragon was shot with an arrow and died, but Hera, Queen of the Gods, was so saddened by his killing, she sent his spirit to the heavens so Draco could guard over the earth. Proud and noble, protective and guarded, Dragons play the hero whenever there is a need for one. But with great power and passion, comes fire. Sometimes moody, sometimes fierce, sometimes intensely playful, a Dragon can make a girl's head spin with all his changes.

Osiris—Sign of the Zombie

In modern times in the West, we have come to know this particular constellation found on the celestial equator as Orion, but to the ancient Egyptians it represented Osiris, the lord of the dead. It makes sense, then, that Zombies, who are ruled by this sign, tend to be strong, silent types. According to legend, Osiris was tricked into a box and thrown into a river where he drowned, so a fear of water is natural to Zombies. Although homebodies, Zombies hate to feel trapped (that box again), so give your man plenty of room to run (and chase). Perhaps because they are governed by the lord of the dead, Zombies are often melancholy, but it's nothing a few hours in front of the Xbox won't cure. Osiris liked his flashy crown adorned with two large ostrich feathers, so let your Zombie dude indulge his own eccentric sense of style.

Quadratus—Sign of the Angel

All Angels are created under the Quadratus constellation, which is made up of the four stars known as Regulus, Fomalhaut, Aldebaran, and

Antares. They form a perfect rectangle and represent the four corners of the universe they guard. Is it any wonder that your Angel is a little bit of a "square?" A square is perfect, but can also be a little boring, and since Angels are the oldest of all the immortals, they can be a little stuck in their ways. There's little room for mistakes with Angels—they rarely make them and can be intolerant of those who do. But age has mellowed them somewhat, and what used to cause them to flare into vengeance now usually provokes a serious talking to at worst.

The Demon Star—Sign of the Demon

Demons are not ruled by a constellation (or anything else), but are deeply affected by the star Algol in the constellation Perseus, found in the northern sky. Algol's other name is the Demon Star, sometimes depicted as the head of Medusa. From the time of the ancients, Algol's brightness would suddenly change, giving a winking effect to Medusa's eye and promoting Demon's playfully evil nature. He may be out for a good time, but this shouldn't be confused with having a good nature. A Demon's soul is as dark as a starless sky.

Your Otherworldly Astrologer

Now that you've got the 4-1-1 on what governs the immortals you love, here's a little bit about your own celestial destiny—and how your stars might align with his.

Aries–The Ram
(March 21–April 20)

You are independent, forceful, and ruled by instinct. You charge ahead without always thinking the consequences through, and because of this, you will live a fuller, more complete life if you avoid relationships with alpha species, such as the Vamps, Dragons, and Demons—but most especially the Angels. You think you are always right, but the Angel knows he is, and the quest to prove yourself would never end. Zombies are the best immortal for your dating satisfaction. You like to lead, and he likes to follow. But don't discount the hunting Werewolf—so long as he's not the pack Alpha—as his absence at night will give you the freedom you crave.

Taurus–The Bull
(April 21–May 21)

You are known for your wisdom, determination, and stubborn core. You trust your instincts—even your most primal, animal ones—and that's a very good thing! They rarely let you down. You love natural foods, heady wines, and physically intense sex. Dating-wise, you have a smorgasbord of choices. Pick any type of immortal *except* a Demon. Those hellish fiends are unchangeable, and your inability to let a project go will bring only heartache.

Gemini–The Twins
(May 22–June 21)

You possess a curious and creative nature. You are constantly on the lookout for passion and adventure, but there are two sides to you. You can burn hot one minute and bluster with cold the next, which means you can lose interest in a project very quickly. That's why you need an immortal who challenges you, one who has lived a dozen lifetimes such as a Vamp, Were, or Demon. Every day will seem exciting and new with these guys. You are least compatible with the Dragons. Their fiery tempers will completely set you off, and you'll find it hard to cool down.

Cancer–The Crab
(June 22–July 22)

You are a nurturer, and while that's a wonderful thing, your inherent sweetness hides your vulnerability and need to be loved in return. You place the well-being of others above your own, and because of that, you need an immortal to look past your smiles and give you the comfort and support you deserve. While you might find yourself drawn to the poor, misunderstood Demon, he will most likely see you as a friend with benefits. Resist the urge to make his world a better place—he likes a hot mess. As Dragons are fierce protectors, these fire-breathers will guard the gift of your heart and find your tenderness the perfect balm for his beast within.

Leo–The Lion
(July 23–August 23)

You are a diva—fabulous, baby! You are full of theatrics and big dreams, and believe you deserve the best that life has to offer, and guess what? You're right! You are strong, fierce, and brave. Demons are feverishly attracted to your flair for drama and love of excitement, but they work for you only in the short term. Their idea of fidelity and your idea of fidelity will never truly align. You need a more stable male. So, forget the old adage about cats and dogs fighting. Werewolves value loyalty as much as you do, and besides that, you'll have a scratch-fest of fun marking each other's territory. You might also find happily-ever-after with an immortal who respects your strength and ferocity, such as a Vamp or a Dragon.

Virgo–The Maiden
(August 24–September 23)

You tend to shy away from casual flings, but you also fear commitment—a sometimes confusing cocktail. You are filled with hope and always see the best in others. You are a helper and will defend anyone in need, even at your own expense. Demons with a secret yearning for grace will flock to you—and you know what? You might be just what a Demon needs in order to be faithful, and he might be what you need to get over your wariness. Demons aren't afraid to pour on the seductive charm, and they will find you a delightful challenge. You might seem more compatible with the Angels, but if paired with a heavenly winger, you run the risk of a life lacking passion and adventure.

Libra–The Balance
(September 24–October 23)

You believe in the importance of justice and that no crime should go unpunished. You hate cruelty of any kind and will always be an advocate of protecting the weaker of the species. While your need to reform your soul mate might seem like a worthwhile venture, you will never be happy if every moment of your life is spent correcting the mistakes of another. So . . . do yourself a favor and avoid the Demons; they're just too wicked for your heart to handle. Seek out a heavenly Angel and go for the gold ring!

Scorpio–The Scorpion
(October 24–November 22)

Unraveling mysteries is your thing, and while you enjoy hiding your emotions from others, you hate when others hide theirs from you. You are extremely passionate yet you rarely allow yourself to fall in love. But when you do give your heart, you're in for the

long haul. While Demons might have the strength to break through your barriers, they aren't likely to stick around. A Zombie might be your best bet for a date, because you want to keep your true desires and wishes hidden, and he'll let you! Also keep the Werewolf in mind. He'll understand your need for loyalty and will never give you reason to worry.

Sagittarius–The Archer
(November 23–December 21)

The thrill of the hunt is what you crave! Whether you're hunting for freedom, the ultimate party, or the love of your life, you charge full steam ahead and the rewards are substantial. You're full of energy, which can sometimes cause you to be impatient with those who are not, and that means you need an undead mate who can last all night. Vamps and Dragons are for you, but don't be surprised if your love of fun has the Demons calling—and your adventurous spirit may be enough to keep that Demon hanging around for eternity. You're least compatible with Angels and Zombies, as they will never be able to keep up with you and might come to resent your wild ways.

Capricorn–The Goat
(December 22–January 20)

You are steady and confident and others flock to you for leadership. You are practical, level-headed, and you like to plan every aspect of your life. This rarely leaves room for spontaneity. You need an immortal who will either push you out of your comfort zone or cater to your need for independence. Or, maybe even a man who will do both—such as a Werewolf. He needs a woman who isn't fazed by his changes or threatened by his long hours away on the nights of the full moon, and he'll always give as good as he gets. Be wary of Demons, who are bound to find you hard to resist and try to stun your sensibilities. A Zombie might appreciate your steadiness, but you run the risk of becoming bored. A great choice for you is a Dragon, who will know he can rant and rave without freaking you out, or a Vamp, who appreciates that you're totally cool with his past (as long as it stays in the past).

Aquarius–The Water Carrier
(January 21–February 19)

You are the original rebel and you're not afraid to shake things up. You are pas-

sionate, yet you place knowledge above emotion. Your interests are wide and varied, but sometimes in your quest for truth, you hurt the feelings of others. The good news is, you always make up for it. Your ideal immortal is one who believes honesty is the best policy. Angels are the top contenders for your heart, though you do well with Dragons and Weres. Zombies are best avoided, as they have trouble handling the truth.

Pisces–The Fish
(February 20—March 20)

You know there is more to life than money and power. You tend to see the best in others while ignoring the danger around you, always going with the flow. Denial is your best friend, and perhaps that's why you are so easy to get along with. At first glance, your best romantic bet seems to be the easygoing Zombie. However, secretly your soul craves someone to take you away from your plain, ordinary life, and the Vamp might be just the immortal to do it . . . as long as he's willing to do most of the work. A Were, Dragon, or Demon would ultimately break your heart, but an Angel could very well understand the treasure you are. ❖

All rights reserved. The reproduction, transmission or utilization of this work in whole or in part in any form by any electronic, mechanical or other means, now known or hereafter invented, including xerography, photocopying and recording, or in any information storage or retrieval system, is forbidden without the written permission of the publisher. For permission please contact Harlequin Enterprises Limited, 225 Duncan Mill Road, Don Mills, Ontario, Canada, M3B 3K9.

This work is a parody. References to any corporation, any product or any individual (whether living, dead or undead) are strictly for purposes of the parody, and no license or authorization has been granted or should be inferred.

Library of Congress Cataloging-in-Publication Data

Showalter, Gena.
Dating the undead / Gena Showalter and Jill Monroe.
    p. cm.
ISBN 978-0-373-89252-5
1. Dating (Social customs)—Humor. 2. Immortalism—Humor. 3. Magazines—Humor. I. Monroe, Jill. II. Title.
PN6231.D3S54 2011
818'.602--dc23

2011024627

® and TM are trademarks owned and used by the trademark owner and/or its licensee. Trademarks indicated with ® are registered in the United States Patent and Trademark Office, the Canadian Trade Marks Office and/or other countries.

www.eharlequin.com

Printed in U.S.A.

Photo Credits

p. 1 Masterfile RF; p. 3 Beauty Photo Studio/age fotostock; p. 3 iStockphoto.com/ Dmitry Mordvintsev; p. 4 Kupka/age fotostock; p. 4 iStockphoto.com/Rick Grant; p. 4 FRANCK CAMHI-VISION/age fotostock; p. 5 Shalom Ormsby/age fotostock; p. 5 © Eric Harvey Brown ; p. 5 Blend Images/Masterfile; p. 6 Ron Fehling/Masterfile; p. 6 © Oleksiy Maksymenko/Alamy; p. 6 iStockphoto.com/Geber86; p. 7 iStockphoto.com/Lauri Patterson; p. 7 iStockphoto.com/Maksim Shmeljov; p. 7 iStockphoto.com/sololos; p. 7 iStockphoto.com/alexzeca; p. 8 Kim Haynes Photos; p. 8 Lauren Floyd; p. 9 iStockphoto.com/Magnilion; p. 10 Tyler Durden/Masterfile; p. 11 iStockphoto.com/ elkor; p. 11 Ben Welsh/age fotostock; p. 11 iStockphoto.com/misterelements ; p. 12 FRANCK CAMHI-VISION/age fotostock; p. 12 ©Corbis Cusp/Alamy; p. 13 Matthew Wiley/ Masterfile; p. 13 iStockphoto.com/bulentgultek ; p. 13 iStockphoto.com/ carolthacker; p. 14 Glow Décor/Masterfile; p. 14 iStockphoto.com/Antagain; p. 15 © Woman/Alamy; p. 16 © Everett Collection Inc. /Alamy; p. 16 © Allstar Picture Library/Alamy; p. 16 © Allstar Picture Library/Alamy; p. 17 © Presselect/Alamy; p. 17 Mattoni/age fotostock; p. 17 © Allstar Picture Library/Alamy ; p. 18 ClassicStock/ Masterfile; p. 18 © David O. Bailey/Alamy; p. 19 © Corbis Flirt/Alamy; p. 19 © nagelestock.com/Alamy; p. 19 © Ron Niebrugge/Alamy; p. 20 Yuri Arcurs/age fotostock; p. 22 © avatra images/Alamy ; p. 22 © Zoonbar GmbH/Alamy; p. 22 iStockphoto.com/ Ugurhan Betin; p. 23 iStockphoto.com/galanter; p. 23 iStockphoto.com/Olena Kuznetsova; p. 23 © Corbis Flirt/Alamy; p. 23 iStockphoto.com/cglade; p. 24 iStockphoto.com/Igor Dutina; p. 25 iStockphoto.com/Elena Elisseeva; p. 25 iStockphoto.com/Nick Garrad; p. 26 iStockphoto.com/eyewave; p. 26 iStockphoto. com/Kasiam; p. 27 © Corbis Cusp/Alamy; p. 28 PBNJ Productions/age fotostock; p. 28 © Corbis Cusp/Alamy; p. 29 Shalom Ormsby/age fotostock; p. 29 Marcos Welsh/age fotostock; p. 29 davide cerati/age fotostock; p. 29 iStockphoto.com/ranplett; p. 30 Kupka/age fotostock; p. 32 © Anka Larazova/Alamy; p. 33 Mirko Iannace/age fotostock; p. 34 Ben Welsh/age fotostock; p. 34 iStockphoto.com/Sasha Xro; p. 35 Graham French/Masterfile; p. 35 iStockphoto.com/ subhandworks; p. 36 Chad Johnson/ Masterfile; p. 37 Rademacher/age fotostock; p. 38 iStockphoto.com/arsenik; p. 38 iStockphoto.com/luchcogs ; p. 39 iStockphoto.com/liseganger ; p. 39 iStockphoto. com/galanter; p. 40 Blend Images/Masterfile ; p. 43 © Oredia/Alamy; p. 43 Natelle/ Shutterstock; p. 44 © Oleksiy Maksymenko Photography/Alamy; p. 44 © Eric Harvey Brown; p. 45 © Trigger Image/Alamy; p. 47 © Stever Gorton/Getty Images; p. 47 © Jewelry specialist/Alamy; p. 48 SEED9/Masterfile; p. 49 Tom Feiler/Masterfile; p. 49 iStockphoto.com/TopsyKretts; p. 50 iStockphoto.com/akvlv; p. 50 © Agencja FREE/ Alamy; p. 52 Arkadius Kozero/age fotostock; p. 52 © Svetlana Saratova/Veer; p. 53 Hiep Vu/age fotostock; p. 54 © Miguel Sobreira/Alamy; p. 54 iStockphoto.com/ misterelements ; p. 56 Masterfile; p. 58 Lucenet Patrice/age fotostock; p. 58 Kablonk!/ age fotostock; p. 59 BEW Authors/age fotostock; p. 59 Lajusticia Richard/age fotostock; p. 59 John Feingersh/age fotostock; p. 60 Mikro Iannace/age fotostock; p. 61 © Glowimages RM/Alamy; p. 61 iStockphoto.com/djFoss; p. 61 iStockphoto.com/ AdShooter; p. 62 FOTOSEARCH RM/age fotostock; p. 64 Ben Welsh/age fotostock; p. 64 Tom Feiler/Masterfile ; p. 65 Sitade/age fotostock; p. 65 Justin Horrocks/age fotostock; p. 65 iStockphoto.com/Living Images; p. 65 iStockphoto.com/Dmitry Mordvintsev; p. 65 iStockphoto.com/PLAINVIEW; p. 65 iStockphoto.com/Dawid Kasza; p. 65 © Chris Rout/Alamy; p. 66 pzAxe/Shutterstock; p. 66 Jaco van Rensburg/Shutterstock; p. 67 Westend61/Masterfile; p. 68 Ron Fehling/Masterfile; p. 69 Masterfile RF; p. 70 Emil Pozar/ age fotostock; p. 70 iStockphoto.com/gkrobar; p. 70 Michael Goldman/Masterfile; p. 71 Blend Images/Masterfile; p. 71 iStockphoto.com/Thirteen-Fifty; p. 71 Cultura RM/ Masterfile; p. 71 STONEIMAGES/age fotostock; p. 71 iStockphoto.com/bulentgultek;

p. 72 © Oleksiy Maksymenko/Alamy; p. 73 iStockphoto.com/maxuser; p. 73 Ramzi Hachicho/Shutterstock; p. 73 Leigh Prather/Shutterstock; p. 74 Baloncici/Shutterstock; p. 74 © Corbis Cusp/Alamy; p. 75 © Laetitia Perrot/Alamy; p. 86 Hajo/age fotostock; p. 87 Sara's Photo Creations; p. 95 BEW Authors/age fotostock; p. 95 iStockphoto.com/Olena Kuznetsova; p. 96 iStockphoto.com/JohnPitcher; p. 97 Cusp and Flirt/Masterfile; p. 98 Ben Welsh/age fotostock; p. 100 Peter Griffith/Masterfile; p. 100 iStockphoto.com/ losw; p. 101 iStockphoto.com/losw; p. 101 Nick Fingerhut/age fotostock; p. 102 iStockphoto.com/losw; p. 102 Peter Griffith/Masterfile; p. 102 Nick Fingerhut/age fotostock; p. 103 iStockphoto.com/marekuliasz; p. 103 © Brad Miller/Alamy; p. 105 iStockphoto.com/Geber86; p. 106 Sarah Murray/Masterfile; p. 107 Westend61/ Masterfile; p. 108 Siephoto/Masterfile; p. 109 iStockphoto.com/Kemter; p. 110 iStockphoto.com/Beboy_ltd; p. 111 iStockphoto.com/anouchka; p. 112 iStock-photo.com/wrangle; p. 113 iStockphoto.com/Geber86; p. 114 Eyecandy Pro/Masterfile; p. 115 Masterfile RF; p. 116 Greg Gerla/age fotostock; p. 117 Masterfile; p. 117 iStockphoto.com/cstar55; p. 118 iStockphoto.com/luchcogs ; p. 118 Andres Rodriguez/age fotostock; p. 119 Aflo Sport/Masterfile; p. 119 Charlie Borland/age fotostock; p. 120 © Frances M. Roberts/Alamy; p. 120 © Photas Ltd/Alamy; p. 121 Aurora Photos/Masterfile; p. 121 Ron Nickel/age fotostock; p. 122 Ben + Marcos Welsh/age fotostock; p. 123 iStockphoto.com/Jill Chen; p. 123 iStockphoto.com/Jack Puccio; p. 123 © Bon Appetit/Alamy; p. 124 iStockphoto.com/Elnur Arnikishiyev; p. 124 iStockphoto.com/martinturzak; p. 125 Yuri Acurs/age fotostock; p. 125 iStockphoto. com/Elenathewise; p. 126 © Oleksiy Maksymenko Photography/Alamy; p. 127 iStockphoto.com/Julie Vader; p. 128 iStockphoto.com/Robert Linton; p. 129 iStockphoto.com/TheCrimsonMonkey; p. 129 iStockphoto.com/YinYang; p. 130 Astrid Lenz/Shutterstock; p. 131 iStockphoto.com/Lauri Patterson; p. 132 iStock-photo.com/Serghei Platonov; p. 133 iStockphoto.com/Rebecca Ellis; p. 133 iStockphoto.com/Rick Grant; p. 134 iStockphoto.com/Boris Ryzhkov; p. 135 iStockphoto.com/William Berry; p. 135 iStockphoto.com/Robert Payne; p. 136 © Retro Kitsch/Alamy; p. 137 © Glowimages RM/Alamy; p. 138 © Tomas Houda/Alamy; p. 139 © Maksim Shemljov/Alamy; p. 140 Cusp and Flirt/Masterfile ; p. 140 Mark Leibowitz/ Masterfile; p. 140 Aurelie and Morgan Da/age fotostock; p. 141 Kevin Dodge/Masterfile; p. 141 Brian Kuhlmann/Masterfile; p. 141 Masterfile RF; p. 142 Masterfile RF; p. 144 iStockphoto.com/aimintang; p. 145 iStockphoto.com/timhughes; p. 146 Blend Images/Masterfile ; p. 146 iStockphoto.com/alerapaso; p. 146 Stefano Cellai/age fotostock ; p. 146 Rodolgo Benitez/age fotostock; p. 147 iStockphoto.com/alerapaso; p. 147 Marcus Lund/age fotostock; p. 147 Darren Greenwood/age fotostock; p. 147 © itanistock/Alamy ; p. 148 Janet Bailey/Masterfile; p. 148 iStockphoto.com/ magnetcreative; p. 149 © Derek Croucher/Alamy; p. 150 © Ron Niebrugge/Alamy; p. 150 © Alaska Stock/Alamy; p. 150 © Stephen Frink Collection/Alamy; p. 151© Arctic-Images/ Alamy; p. 151 © Craig Richardson/Alamy; p. 151 © Rolf Richardson/Alamy; p. 152 © dbimages/Alamy; p. 152 © Viennaslide/Alamy; p. 152 © imagebroker/Alamy; p. 153 © Alain Machet (3) /Alamy; p. 153 © Johnny Grieg/Alamy; p. 153 © pictureproject/Alamy; p. 154 PATRICK FORGET/age fotostock; p. 155 iStockphoto.com/haveseen; p. 155 iStockphoto.com/biffspandex; p. 156 iStockphoto.com/sololos; p. 157 iStockphoto. com/alexzeca; p. 157 iStockphoto.com/vectorcartoons; p. 157 iStockphoto.com/ Jason Murray; p. 157 iStockphoto.com/Dmitriy Chernyshkov; p. 157 iStockphoto. com/bulgentgultek; p. 157 iStockphoto.com/John Takai; p. 158 iStockphoto.com/ Larazev; p. 159 iStockphoto.com/Larazev; IBC PBNJ Productions/age fotostock; IBC iStockphoto.com/nilsz; Back Cover Kim Haynes Photos; Back Cover Lauren Floyd